Transcontinental Books
1100 René-Lévesque Boulevard West
24th floor
Montreal (Quebec) H3B 4X9
Tel.: 514 340-3587
Toll-free 1-866-800-2500
www.livres.transcontinental.ca

Bibliothèque et Archives nationales du Québec and Library and Archives Canada cataloguing in publication

Kennedy, Ryan
Young Guns 2
At head of title: The Hockey News.

ISBN 978-0-9813938-8-9

1. Hockey players - North America - Anecdotes. 2. National Hockey League - Anecdotes.
I. Dixon, Ryan. II. Fraser, Edward, 1978-   . III. Hockey news (Montréal, Québec). IV. Title.

GV848.5.A1K46 2012   796.962'6409227   C2011-942321-9

Head of production: Marie-Suzanne Menier
Proofreading: Ronnie Shuker
Layout: Louise Besner, Diane Marquette
Page design: Annick Désormeaux and Anne-Laure Jean
Cover design and photo editing: Erika Vanderveer

Cover photo credits
Steven Stamkos: Scott Audette/NHLI via Getty Images; Luke Schenn: Graig Abel/NHLI via
Getty Images; Carey Price: G. Fiume/Getty Images; Jonathan Toews (back cover): Bill Smith/
NHLI via Getty Images

Printed in Canada
© Transcontinental Books, 2011
Legal deposit – 4th quarter 2011
National Library of Quebec
National Library of Canada

We acknowledge the financial support of the Government of Canada through the Canada Book
Fund for our publishing activities and the Government of Quebec through the SODEC Tax
Credit for our publishing activities.

For information on special rates for corporate libraries and wholesale purchases,
please call 1-866-800-2500.

HOW 25 WHIZ KIDS REACHED STARDOM

By Ryan Kennedy & Ryan Dixon

Transcontinental Books

For all the incredibly
selfless hockey parents out there
– especially my own. *– RD*

To my wife Christine and my
daughter Elizabeth. Our family
grows together. *– RK*

Introduction

There's no such thing as an overnight success in sports. Even the most fresh-faced professionals have journeyed far from where they began.

The stories you will read in this book are the perfect indicator of this. Despite the fact we are talking about players who, at the oldest, are in their early 20s, the hard work and perseverance they have shown is a true measure of dedication to their craft. Not only that, but the tireless hours and long drives put in by their parents is proof no one makes it alone.

In fact, if a secondary theme is at play here, it would be the relationship between these players and their parents. The NHLers in the pages to follow come from all over the continent and Europe, but the most common threads to be found is the bond shared between the kids and their parents. Hockey basically mandates it.

Carey Price's father flew him to games and practices from remote Anahim Lake in British Columbia. Matt Duchene stays grounded to this day by setting out on fishing expeditions with his father. John Tavares navigated the waters of media hype and pressure with the aid of his mom. P.K. Subban time and again shared late night/early morning pizza with his father after public skates well beyond midnight. The list is lengthy.

Within this group of phenoms is a raft of Calder Trophy winners and first overall draft picks. Some were scouted since the time they were young teenagers, while others emerged later, picking up steam during their draft year and taking off into hockey's stratosphere. A constant, however, is that all will be important contributors to NHL teams for years to come. Some already have Stanley Cup success and All-Star Games to their credit, while others are champing at the bit for the chance.

This is the next wave of the NHL stars; the faces we will see dominate the next decade, until the Young Guns who are just beginning their journey emerge.

Table of Contents

HOCKEY'S YOUNG GUNS

HOCKEY'S FUTURE YOUNG GUNS

HOCKEY'S YOUNG GUNS

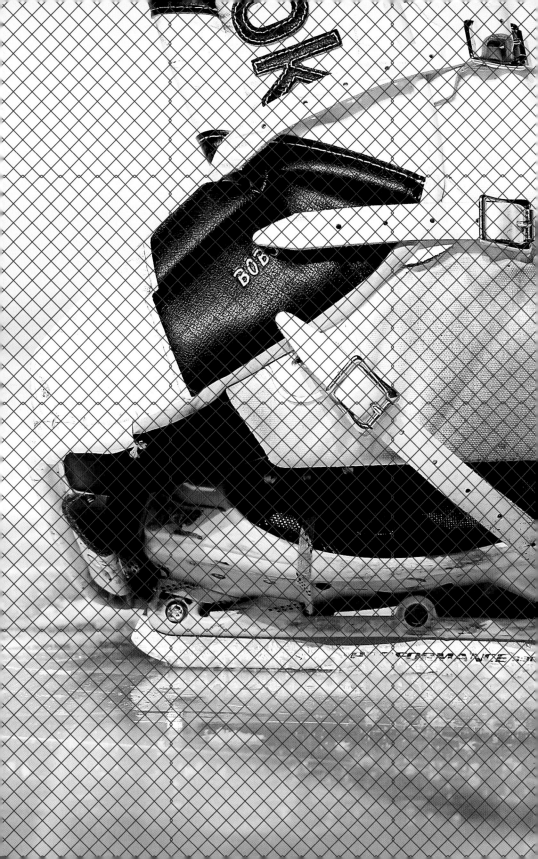

CAREY PRICE

MONTREAL CANADIENS

POSITION: GOALIE
DRAFTED: 5TH OVERALL IN 2005
BORN: AUGUST 16, 1987 – ANAHIM LAKE, B.C.
LAST DEVELOPMENTAL TEAM: TRI-CITY AMERICANS (WHL)

A few facets of Carey Price's journey to the role of starting goalie for the Montreal Canadiens seem taxing. Start with the fact that as a youngster, Carey and his dad spent a significant amount of time travelling by both land and air just to get him to minor hockey games and practices. But instead of wearing him out, those extensive expeditions just molded him into someone who could handle the voyage.

"Driving for me is no big deal," Carey said. "I can jump in a car and drive 10 hours and step out fresh. I feel like I've been putting miles in my whole life."

Carey, along with is younger sister, Kayla, grew up in the remote central British Columbia community of Anahim Lake, which has a population of fewer than 400. That meant that while Carey could play hockey at every turn on frozen ponds and the creek running through the backyard of the Price family home, there was no nearby option for organized hockey.

About the time Carey was eight or nine, his dad, Jerry, realized allowing his son to continue on the hockey journey was going to require some serious commitment.

"It was obvious that if he was going to enjoy hockey any further he was going to have to get involved in a minor hockey program," Jerry said. "That's when we made the decision we'd get him back and forth to Williams Lake to play organized hockey."

Williams Lake is located about 320 kilometers east of Anahim Lake, meaning getting there by car is a bit of a haul. With that in mind, Jerry decided that whenever weather allowed he would put his pilot's license to use and the two would fly back and forth between the two towns.

Once Carey started playing on travel teams, he and his dad were faced with making the trip three times a week. Eventually Jerry secured a residence for the family in Williams Lake so he and Carey could stay over on Wednesday nights in advance of early-morning practices on Thursday. After practice, they'd fly home and Carey would hurry off to school. (Jerry's position as an administrator of an adult learning center gave him some flexibility and he acknowledged Carey was lucky to have some very understanding teachers.)

The flight took about an hour and a half, from loading up the hockey gear to landing. When it wasn't safe to fly, Carey and Jerry would drive, meaning they'd be on the road between three or four hours each way. When the Williams Lake team travelled for road games, it meant another trip from 90 minutes to three hours to a different center.

"I didn't do all of that travelling thinking one day Carey would have a chance to play in the NHL, it was just to give him an opportunity to do something he wanted to." Jerry said. "Not only that, it was something I was involved in and enjoyed being in it with him. It's a lot of driving, but I wouldn't trade a minute of it for anything because we did get to spend a lot of time together. And I don't think Carey would, either."

It was during those long excursions, no doubt, that Jerry passed on a few pointers from his time in the crease. The elder Price played major junior out west and although he never advanced beyond minor pro, he was drafted 126th overall by the Philadelphia Flyers in 1978.

> "I didn't do all of that travelling thinking one day Carey would have a chance to play in the NHL, it was just to give him an opportunity to do something he wanted to."
>
> **– Jerry Price**

While goaltending techniques have obviously evolved immensely over the past 30 years, Jerry could still speak to the between-the-ears element of the crease that never really changes.

"I think his dad did a good job at a young age of coaching him on how you have to think the game," said Don Nachbaur, Carey's Western League coach with the Tri-City Americans.

CAREY PRICE USED TO LITERALLY FLY TO GET TO HOCKEY GAMES WHEN HE WAS A YOUNGSTER, BUT HE'S REALLY TAKEN FLIGHT IN MONTREAL BACKING THE HISTORIC HABS

Nachbaur would know because not only did he coach Carey, he played against Jerry in major junior. Nachbaur's first year as coach of the Americans coincided with Carey's rookie season of 2003-04. Most goalies don't see much time as 16-year-olds in the 'Dub,' but Price played 28 regular season games and got the call to start in the playoffs, where Tri-City

upset the Portland Winter Hawks in Round 1 before losing to the eventual Memorial Cup-champion Kelowna Rockets in the second round.

"He was one of those special guys who came in at 16 and wanted to impact the game," Nachbaur said.

The next year, 2004-05, Carey was eligible for the NHL draft. Because that season coincided with the NHL lockout, Carey also had the unique experience of spending time with an out-of-work world-class goalie.

Washington Capitals puckstopper Olie Kolzig was a silent partner in the Americans ownership group and because there was no NHL hockey going on, the 2000 Vezina Trophy winner was spending some time around the rink in Tri-City. His relationship with Carey wasn't so much about sharing specific tips in terms of technique, but rather just having conversations about the position in general and how to stay focused in the crease. There was also room for a little fun.

"He liked to joke around after practice," Kolzig said. "He'd tend to drop the gloves and spar a little bit."

Carey clearly relished the chance to keep company with someone who had already achieved exactly what he was after.

"There aren't too many times you get to hang out with an all-star goalie as a junior," Carey said.

After Montreal picked him fifth overall in 2005, Carey's star really started to rise. In January of 2007, he helped lead Team Canada to gold at the World Junior Championship in Sweden. Carey posted a perfect 6-0-0 mark with a miniscule 1.14 goals-against average at the event, which was defined in many ways by his performance – along with that of future Chicago Blackhawks captain Jonathan Toews – in a semifinal shootout victory over the United States.

Under international rules, players are allowed to make multiple attempts and Toews was the goal-scoring hero, while Carey made big save after big save to give Canada the win.

> ## "He liked to joke around after practice. He'd tend to drop the gloves and spar a little bit."
>
> ## – Olie Kolzig

"To this day, it's probably the most nervous I've been playing hockey," he said.

Just months later, Carey stormed the pro scene, winning playoff MVP honors while leading the American League's Hamilton Bulldogs to a Calder Cup championship at the tender age of 19.

The following fall, he was handpicked by Canadiens GM Bob Gainey to make the big team in training camp. Good as he was, Carey's selection startled many who thought he still needed more time in the minors.

During his first three years in hockey-mad Montreal, Carey experienced his shares of highs and lows, including some tension-filled exchanges with fans. Carey acknowledged the super-charged atmosphere surrounding the Canadiens and the pressure of being a No. 1 stopper at such a young age was initially a bit much to handle for a young man from such a small community.

"You get a kid coming out of junior hockey who has lived with a billet family," he said, "then you give him a whole bunch of money and free reign to do whatever he wants in a huge city like Montreal; it can be a little overwhelming. It takes time to learn how to be a professional and manage yourself."

For Jerry, it hasn't always been easy watching his son work through the growing pains.

"I told somebody one time who asked me, 'What do you think when they're booing Carey?' and I said, 'Well, what would you think if they booed your daughter off the stage in the school play?' " he said. "You're not angry with the fans necessarily, but you're very aware of what impact it might have on your child. It's a helpless feeling because you want to protect them and there's nothing you can do other than try to help them pick up the pieces when they're finished."

Perhaps the turning point for Carey was in the spring of 2010 when Jaroslav Halak's stellar play led the Canadiens on a deep playoff run. After the season, some thought Carey might be traded given Halak's emergence, but the Habs maintained faith in the 6-foot-3 B.C. boy and instead dealt Halak to the St. Louis Blues.

Carey responded with a terrific season in which he re-established himself as one of the premier young creasemen in the game. Kolzig believes the turmoil Carey has endured may have crushed some green goalies, but he believes Price is now better off for having gone through those tough times all before the age of 24.

"He's the perfect goaltender for the Montreal Canadiens because of his ability to deal with pressure, scrutiny, expectations," Kolzig said.

Part of that is because of the characteristics Carey inherited from his mom, Lynda. While Jerry may have passed on the easygoing manner, Carey also benefited from the fact his mother is prominent in central B.C.'s aboriginal community and at one point held the role of chief of the Ulkatcho Indian Band.

"My mom is a strong person and a leader and I think those types of things rubbed off on me," Carey said. "Being in the position I'm in, I need to have that, so she's really had a good influence on me."

Carey's main focus right now is helping the Canadiens become one of the league's elite teams. Though he's already put a lot of miles behind him to get where he is, he remains excited about the road ahead in Montreal.

"When we're winning, there's absolutely no better place to play in any sport, I'll guarantee you that." – *Ryan Dixon*

★★★★★★★★★★★★★★★★★★★★★★★★★★★★★★★★★★★

**CAREY PRICE'S FAVORITE [...]
GROWING UP**

PLAYERS: CURTIS JOSEPH, MARTIN BRODEUR, PATRICK ROY
JERSEY: VANCOUVER CANUCKS (RED ALTERNATE)
CARTOON: THE BUGS BUNNY AND TWEETY SHOW
MUSICIAN: ERIC CHURCH
MOVIE: TOMBSTONE
SCHOOL SUBJECTS: SOCIAL STUDIES AND PHYS-ED
JUNK FOOD: MINI EGGS

★★★★★★★★★★★★★★★★★★★★★★★★★★★★★★★★★★★

TAYLOR HALL

EDMONTON OILERS

POSITION: LEFT WING
DRAFTED: 1ST OVERALL IN 2010
BORN: NOVEMBER 14, 1991 – CALGARY, ALTA.
LAST DEVELOPMENTAL TEAM: WINDSOR SPITFIRES (OHL)

Sure, Edmonton Oilers left winger Taylor Hall was pushed around in a bobsleigh as a youngster, but you wouldn't find him zipping down the chute at the same speeds as his father did with the Canadian national team.

"You had to be a certain age to go down the bobsleigh track," Taylor said. "And by that time, I was too serious about hockey for me to go risking my life."

So instead of flying down an icy hill, Hall decided to continue soaring down the sheets of ice – and the rest is history.

Taylor's father, Steve Hall, played in the Canadian Football League before turning his interests to bobsleigh. Living in Calgary, all the amenities were there thanks to the 1988 Olympics. But Taylor's passion always resided in hockey.

"My memories are of him just always wanting to go play," said Taylor's mom, Kim Strba. "His father built a rink in the backyard every winter and the kids in the neighborhood would all come over every day. That's the type of unorganized hockey where they can get very creative."

Which has clearly paid off in the long run for Taylor. Ever since he joined the Ontario League as a 15-year-old, Taylor has been dazzling folks with his great skill and goal-scoring acumen. Funny to think then, how major junior history might have changed if the Hall family had remained in Calgary and Taylor been drafted into the Western League.

TAYLOR HALL'S FATHER PLAYED PRO FOOTBALL AND WAS ALSO A BOBSLEDDER. BUT YOU WON'T FIND TAYLOR FLYING DOWN ANY ICY CHUTES – HOCKEY IS TOO IMPORTANT.

But as it was, Taylor, then 13, and his family moved to Kingston, Ont., where Kim's six brothers and sisters lived. It was a different experience for the teen, but he got to Kingston on a Thursday and had a hockey team and a new best friend by Friday. Still, it was tough to say goodbye to Calgary.

"He didn't want to go," Kim said. "He took one for the team there. It could have been make-or-break for a teenage boy, but he handled it very well."

In Kingston, Hall's game continued to grow and soon it was on to the OHL's Windsor Spitfires. Being born in November, Hall was still 15 when his OHL experience began, but that didn't stop him from making an immediate impact. The Spitfires were beginning to come on as a juggernaut and Hall did his share by pumping in 45 goals as a freshman, leading the team in that category. Not too shabby, considering the Spits also featured future New York Islander Josh Bailey, who rang up 96 points that campaign.

> "All those coaches in Windsor, they formed me into the player I am today."
>
> **– Taylor Hall**

Despite a great season, Windsor also tasted tragedy that year. On February 18, 2008, captain Mickey Renaud collapsed at his home and died. A hometown hero and Calgary Flames draft pick, the 19-year-old had a genetic heart disease known as hypertrophic cardiomyopathy, which often goes undetected until it's too late. The loss in Windsor was very difficult for all involved.

"All the parents came for the week to take care of their kids," Kim said. "That's the first time Taylor had dealt with anything like that. I still get emotional thinking about that time."

The Mickey Renaud tragedy was a big story in Canada and certainly a transformative event for the Spitfires franchise. Though the loss of their captain and friend was tough, the Spits didn't take long to honor his commitment.

The very next season Windsor rode Taylor, defenseman Ryan Ellis and Calgary pick Greg Nemisz all the way to the Memorial Cup tournament. After clinching the OHL crown, the Spits didn't make things easy for themselves, however.

The team dropped the first two games of the tourney before becoming the first team to win the title after opening with a pair of losses.

Windsor met Kelowna, the Western League champ, in the final and the Rockets were no pushovers, featuring future NHLers Tyler Myers, Mikael Backlund and Jamie Benn.

With everything on the line, the Spitfires came out flying. Windsor scored on its first three shots of the game and ultimately won 4-1. Taylor had just one assist, but was still named the game's first star for his efforts.

Windsor would return to the Memorial Cup the next season as well, trouncing the host Brandon Wheat Kings 9-1 in the title match.

"Maybe the second one was more gratifying," Taylor said. "Because we won so convincingly."

But he was also quick to point out that the Spits nearly didn't even make it to that second Memorial Cup. During the OHL playoffs, Windsor ran into Jeff Skinner's Kitchener Rangers and the future Carolina Hurricanes phenom was on a post-season tear. The Rangers took a seemingly insurmountable 3-0 lead in the series before Windsor stormed back to take the battle in seven games.

A little adversity never hurts and Taylor believes that was a challenge that steeled the Spitfires for the road ahead. Overall, he was very pleased with his time in Windsor under the tutelage of coach Bob Boughner and GM Warren Rychel, two former NHLers who also owned the franchise.

"All those coaches there, they formed me into the player I am today," Taylor said.

Passion has never been a problem for Taylor Hall, evidenced by his play at the 2010 World Junior Championship in Saskatchewan.

He also has always gotten advice from his father. With Steve Hall withstanding the rigors of the Canadian Football League schedule and excelling in bobsleigh, he knew what his son needed to do in order to succeed. And though the sport was different, Taylor always listened to what his father had to say about his performance.

"It's pretty hard to see yourself when you're playing," Taylor said. "So it was great having him there."

Taylor's mom also saw the importance of having another elite athlete in the family as her son grew up.

"He saw the dedication that Steve had for his sport," Kim said. "And the passion – that's something you can't teach."

Passion has never been a problem for Taylor, evidenced by his play at the 2010 World Junior Championship in Saskatchewan. The Canadians famously fell to the archrival Americans in a crushing final that went into overtime, but Taylor also proved why he was the frontrunner to go first overall in the NHL draft. He finished the tournament with six goals and 12 points in six games, putting him third overall.

And though most folks assumed Taylor would go first, there were those championing Plymouth's Tyler Seguin as the top prospect – including the NHL's Central Scouting Bureau. Edmonton, which held the first selection, also did a good job of playing coy.

"He didn't know until Edmonton called his name at the podium," Kim said. "The Oilers never tipped their hand."

Naturally, going first overall was a big deal for Taylor.

"At the time I was thinking about it a lot," he said. "What with all the media pressure and all."

Taylor went on to join a young Oilers squad that included fellow rookies Jordan Eberle – a teammate from the world juniors – and young Swedish star Magnus Paajarvi. Being three high-profile freshmen coming in at the same time diffused the pressure for the kids in Edmonton – they were all in the same situation and the focus wouldn't solely be on one of them. Taylor and Jordan lived in the same apartment as rookies, while Magnus was in the same building.

On the ice, everything was still a wakeup call.

"It's not the kind of league you can ease into," Taylor said. "You really have to be prepared."

Though he had just one assist in his first seven NHL games, Taylor followed up with multi-point efforts in the next two outings, including his first NHL goal, in a game against Columbus. But it was those same Blue Jackets who would put a serious cramp in Taylor's rookie campaign. On March 3, after having already tallied a goal and an assist, he got into an ill-advised fight with Jackets tough guy Derek Dorsett. Taylor fell awkwardly in the tilt and injured his ankle. On the bright side, it marked his first Gordie Howe Hat Trick. But the down sides were much greater. Taylor's season was finished, just as he was putting together a run of offense.

"I don't think he was really expecting what (the NHL) was going to be like," Eberle said. "As the year went on, he got really good. He was playing his best hockey until he got injured, which sucked because he would have kept playing really well."

The injury also cost Taylor a shot at playing for Canada at the World Championship, but at least he got to enjoy some fanfare when Edmonton once again owned the first overall selection at the draft in Minnesota. He even got to welcome the newest Oiler, Ryan Nugent-Hopkins, on stage.

"I got a chance to talk to him a little bit," Taylor said. "You can tell he wants to be the best player he can be."

Which sounds like déjà vu for the Oilers. – *Ryan Kennedy*

✦✦✦✦✦✦✦✦✦✦✦✦✦✦✦✦✦✦✦✦✦✦✦✦✦✦✦✦✦✦✦✦

TAYLOR HALL FAVORITE […] GROWING UP

JERSEY: TEAM CANADA
MEMORABILIA: SIGNED BOBBY ORR JERSEY
CARTOON: HEY ARNOLD!
ALBUM: THEORY OF A DEADMAN
BY THEORY OF A DEADMAN
MOVIE: GOOD WILL HUNTING
SCHOOL SUBJECT: GEOGRAPHY
JUNK FOOD: MCDONALD'S

✦✦✦✦✦✦✦✦✦✦✦✦✦✦✦✦✦✦✦✦✦✦✦✦✦✦✦✦✦✦✦✦

JONATHAN TOEWS

CHICAGO BLACKHAWKS

POSITION: CENTER
DRAFTED: 3RD OVERALL IN 2006
BORN: APRIL 29, 1988 – WINNIPEG, MAN.
LAST DEVELOPMENTAL TEAM: NORTH DAKOTA FIGHTING SIOUX (WCHA)

The backyard pond is an iconic place for many Canadians and growing up in Winnipeg, the Toews boys first demonstrated their competitiveness on such a sheet of ice.

"They played a lot of hours on the backyard pond," said Bryan Toews, the father of the clan. "A few times we'd see sticks flying, but no bloody noses, so I guess they figured it out."

Jonathan and David Toews both went on to play the sport at a high level, but the older brother and captain of the Chicago Blackhawks revealed that competition at home would help the brothers abroad.

"He definitely challenged me," Jonathan said. "He was two years younger, so I shouldn't have had to worry, but it was always competitive."

Going through the local youth hockey circuit, Jonathan recalls he and his brother both being at the top of their age groups as they grew up. David was taken in the third round of the 2008 NHL draft by the New York Islanders and followed his older sibling to the University of North Dakota before switching to Brandon of the Western League in 2010-11. Jonathan's path has already led to the highest echelons of hockey – just as he planned.

"For myself, there was no alternative," Jonathan said. "One level after another, you get better."

Jonathan showed promise right from the start. His dad remembers him traipsing through the house in his skates and that passion carried onto the ice.

"He had been skating by the time he was three-and-a-half and had a stride at four," Bryan said. "That blew my mind."

The future Blackhawk first realized around 12 or 13 that he could really do something special in hockey and soon after, that led him to one of several key decisions he made as a teenager. At 15, he decided to pull up stakes in Winnipeg and head down to Minnesota to attend Shattuck-St. Mary's, a prep school whose hockey program had already spun out Sidney Crosby, Zach Parise and Jack Johnson.

"First, we said no way," Bryan recalled. "It was way too young."

But several factors worked in Shattuck's favor in the long run. By attending the school, Jonathan would not only get a great education and continue to play high-level hockey, but he would also be preserving his NCAA eligibility, something that would become very prominent just a few years later.

In the Western League's bantam draft, Jonathan was selected by the Tri-City Americans, a franchise with a great reputation and two former NHLers for owners in Olaf Kolzig and Stu Barnes. But the team was also located in Washington state, pretty much as far away from the Toews' Winnipeg home as possible. That's when the University of North Dakota began to seem like a pretty good alternative.

"It was the WHL until I was 17," Jonathan said. "It was last minute. I loved everything about North Dakota. It was a tough decision because things could have worked out well in Tri-City, too."

But first Toews had to get through his first stretch of life away from home. Shattuck-St. Mary's isn't actually too far from Winnipeg, but it's still eight-plus hours in the car. Plus, Jonathan was going in by himself.

"He didn't know anybody," Bryan said. "Not one soul at that school."

> ## "He had been skating by the time he was three-and-a-half and had a stride at four. That blew my mind."
>
> ## — Bryan Toews

NICKNAMED 'CAPTAIN SERIOUS' IN THE NHL, JONATHAN TOEWS WAS MAKING BIG DECISIONS ABOUT HIS CAREER WHEN HE WAS MUCH YOUNGER.

As with many of the kids who commit to Shattuck's, Jonathan's most important stretch was the first six to eight weeks, when the homesickness is at its worst. But the dorm room atmosphere and the fact players live with their teammates seven days a week eventually turned the group into something close to a family.

And just to make things a little more interesting, Toews combined three years of high school into two so that he could get to the University of North Dakota sooner. He was actually a freshman at 17, playing on one of the best teams in the nation. Despite his young age, Toews excelled as a rookie on the Fighting Sioux, finishing fourth in scoring with 22 goals and 39 points in 42 games. The three players who tallied more points than him – Drew Stafford, Travis Zajac and T.J. Oshie – are all impact players in the NHL now and a couple years older.

"Jonathan thought he could do it," Bryan said. "But we thought, 'Man, he's playing against men there.' "

But being nearly a point-per-game player at a top school will get you noticed in a lot of corners and Toews was no exception. Heading into the 2006 draft, his name was being bandied about as a player to watch near the top.

"When you hear people talk for a year-and-a-half, two years about you going high, you wonder," Jonathan said.

On draft day, St. Louis opted to take big U.S. national team development program defenseman Erik Johnson with the first selection. While that wasn't much of a shock, there was uncertainty in pick No. 2, which belonged to Pittsburgh. Jonathan thought he was going to become a Penguin, but the honor went to Peterborough center Jordan Staal instead. That's when the nerves kicked in.

"I really thought when Pittsburgh took Staal that I might slide down to sixth or seventh," Toews said. "But going to Chicago third, I think I was the luckiest guy that day."

Which, at the time, seemed a little crazy. After all, despite having the second pick, Pittsburgh was already armed with Sidney Crosby, Evgeni Malkin and Marc-Andre Fleury, while the Hawks had...well, nothing. But the venerable franchise, mired in its status as a laughingstock at the time, was not far from better days.

Though it would have been tempting to leave school behind, Jonathan went back to Grand Forks and had another stellar season with the Fighting Sioux, winning a World Junior Championship with Canada in the middle. He led his country in scoring with seven points in six games at the tourney, where he squared off against Team USA star and future running mate Patrick Kane. Both were named tournament all-stars by the media.

Kane was the first pick overall in 2007, but made the leap straight to the NHL that year. Toews joined him and the pair was locked at the hip from the very beginning.

With no expectations in Chicago, the two burgeoning stars were allowed to grow organically and had a coach in Denis Savard who knew what it was like to be an elite talent in the game.

> **"When Jordan Staal won the Cup, I asked Jonathan if he would have rather gone to Pittsburgh. He said, 'Nope, we're going to win it here.' "**
>
> **– Bryan Toews**

"He understood what it takes for a player to get comfortable," Jonathan said. "It's tough for a skill player not to get minutes when you're young."

But Savard gave his charges that opportunity and they rewarded him. Kane went on the win the Calder Trophy as rookie of the year, while Toews established himself as a young leader on the team.

In fact, Toews was such a respected player in the Blackhawks room that he was named captain of the team beginning in 2008-09. He was just a sophomore in the NHL at the time and only 20. But his ability to impact a squad became obvious very quickly.

Savard had been replaced behind the bench by Joel Quenneville and with defenders Duncan Keith and Brent Seabrook joining Toews and Kane as serious building blocks, the Hawks were suddenly a force to be reckoned with. Chicago made the playoffs for the first time in six seasons and pushed all the way to the Western Conference final, where the Hawks were dusted by Detroit.

But the next season brought even greater fortune. Marian Hossa, who had played for the Red Wings the year prior and was still searching for a Stanley Cup after two straight losses in the final, chose Chicago as the best place to end his quest. In a magical season, the Hawks slayed the dragon that was Detroit, snatching the Central Division title from their rival and securing the second seed in the West.

This time, no one could stop Chicago. The Blackhawks swept the West's top-seeded San Jose Sharks in the conference final and wrestled the Cup from Philadelphia in a six-game classic that featured one of the strangest Cup-winning goals ever – one that Kane saw go in off his own stick, but most others did not until seconds later.

Not only did Toews, as captain, become the first Chicago Blackhawk in 49 years to hoist the Stanley Cup, but he also got a measure of closure on his slight draft day slide.

"When Staal won the Cup, I asked him if he would have rather gone to Pittsburgh," Bryan recalled. "And he said, 'Nope, we're going to win it here.' "

Jonathan was right on the money there, but he's far from satisfied with just one victory. The next season saw a Hawks team depleted due to the salary cap, but still feisty. Chicago stormed back from a 3-0 deficit to force Vancouver into a Game 7 overtime situation in the first round of the playoffs, only to fall short by that one most crucial tally. But the team is still young and, most importantly, has Toews and his buddy Kane in the fold.

"We definitely want to do it again," Jonathan said. – *Ryan Kennedy*

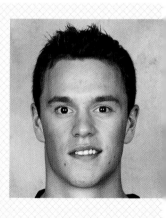

★★★★★★★★★★★★★★★★★★★★★★★★★★★★★★★★★

JONATHAN TOEWS FAVORITE [...] GROWING UP

MEMORABILIA: LOS ANGELES KINGS WAYNE GRETZKY JERSEY (SIGNED BY PLAYERS LIKE MARTY MCSORLEY AND KELLY HRUDEY, BUT NOT GRETZKY)
CARTOON: LOONEY TUNES
MUSICIAN: JASON ALDEAN
MOVIE: THE PURSUIT OF HAPPYNESS
VIDEO GAME: CALL OF DUTY
SCHOOL SUBJECT: FRENCH
JUNK FOOD: CHOCOLATE

★★★★★★★★★★★★★★★★★★★★★★★★★★★★★★★★★

LOGAN COUTURE

SAN JOSE SHARKS

POSITION: CENTER
DRAFTED: 9TH OVERALL IN 2007
BORN: MARCH 28, 1989 – GUELPH, ONT.
LAST DEVELOPMENTAL TEAM: OTTAWA 67'S (OHL)

Logan Couture was already feeling pretty good when the big news came.

Not yet a full month into the start of his pro career with the American League's Worcester Sharks, Logan was already glimpsing the potential the San Jose Sharks saw when the club made him its first pick in 2007.

Case in point: On the night of Oct. 24, 2009, the visiting Springfield Falcons played Worcester to a scoreless draw through three periods, despite being outshot 44-16. The Sharks kept coming in overtime and when they finally found a crack in the armor of Falcons goalie Devan Dubnyk, it was Logan who fired the game-winner. Worcester was smack in the middle of a classic three-game AHL weekend and with a tilt in Hartford the next afternoon on the horizon, Logan didn't have a lot of time to celebrate; he just wanted to get some rest before the next game. Then came news the site of that contest might be on a bigger stage.

"The GM in Worcester called me into his office and said, 'There've been some injuries up top, keep your phone on tonight. We might call you, you could be going up, we're not sure yet,' " Logan said. "I went home, waited, waited and I got the call around (midnight), they told me I was going up. I called my parents and they were all excited."

After a 4 a.m. wake-up call to make a flight from Boston to Philadelphia, Logan slept all day then headed to the rink. The night every young hockey player dreams about was finally here and he didn't even have to wait for the action to begin for his welcome-to-the-big-leagues moment.

"I remember walking out for warmups and in the American League there's 50 to 100 people in the stands watching, but in the NHL there's probably 5,000 people and the lights are so bright, the music was loud and it was just unbelievable," he said.

That Logan ever had the chance to step onto NHL ice would come as a surprise to anybody who may have witnessed his first-ever skating experience. Ted Couture was just doing what so many other dads have done before him when he took Logan out to the local rink in London, Ont. The future hockey star didn't exactly embrace it.

"He had a little crying session where he wanted to get off the ice," Ted said. "I think he was four that year. Pretty much all of the other kids were older and more experienced. So they were skating around, moving pretty well, some of them were skating backwards. I think when Logan saw that, he probably thought he was way out of his element, he was scared or whatever and didn't like it."

"In the NHL the lights were so bright, the music was loud – it was just unbelievable."

– Logan Couture

That sentiment changed over time. As a firefighter, Ted often had time off during the day. After a little hiatus following the first failed attempt on blades, he started taking Logan back out for "parents and tots" skating and, sure enough, things started going more smoothly.

The family eventually moved just outside London to the tiny community of Birr and Logan played his youth hockey in the small town of Lucan. Playing in London, a city of about 350,000 people, was an option, but Ted believes spending his early days in Lucan really helped Logan.

"Absolutely, without a doubt," Ted said. "It was beneficial to him, in our opinion, anyway. Playing in a smaller town, the teams are a little bit smaller. The whole atmosphere, from the parent groups to the politics , it was just very stress-free playing in a small town like that."

Towns are assigned a letter rating based on their size and Lucan's population of only a couple thousand people meant it was tagged a DD center. That's why, when the team travelled to Owen Sound, Ont., for a tournament filled with teams from much larger places, with A- and B-level designations, there was a little bit of snickering going on.

"All of the other parents and some of the kids even were laughing when they saw this Lucan team walk into the arena with their DD coats on," Ted recalled. "They were saying, 'What the heck are these guys doing here? We're going to kill them, we're going to feast upon them.' Well, Lucan ended up winning the tournament."

That was in large part due to the fact Logan was really beginning to show what he could do on the ice. Ted recalled one contest where his son was triple-teamed and forced to fight through some hacks and whacks, but still managed to get his goals.

"That particular memory for me stands out probably because it was the best game I've seen him play that I can remember, individually, anyway," he said.

Logan eventually started competing at a higher level of hockey in AAA for the London Junior Knights alongside another future NHLer, Los Angeles Kings defenseman Drew Doughty. It was around that time John Thornton, the brother and agent of Logan's future Sharks teammate Joe Thornton, got a phone call from an Ontario League scout named Mike Taylor.

"He told me, 'You've got to see this kid'," John said. "I went to see him and he was head and shoulders above the rest of the guys."

> **"I went to see Logan and he was head and shoulders above the rest of the guys."**
>
> **– John Thornton**

John is Logan's agent today and the latter followed in Joe's footsteps by playing Jr. B hockey for the St. Thomas Stars. After a good showing as a 15-year-old rookie with 46 points in 48 games, Logan was drafted by the OHL's Ottawa 67's. At the time, Ottawa was guided by major junior coaching legend Brian Kilrea. Playing for 'Killer' is an experience Logan said had a tremendous impact on him, away from the ice as well as on it.

"One thing that he really preaches is respect and that's something that's stuck with me to this day is to respect everyone," Logan said. "You go to a restaurant to eat for a

LOGAN COUTURE FINISHED SECOND IN CALDER VOTING IN 2011. SURELY THE ONLY CHALICE HE – AND ALL SHARKS PLAYERS AND FANS – CARE ABOUT, HOWEVER, IS THE ELUSIVE STANLEY CUP.

pre-game meal and you couldn't leave the restaurant without saying thank you to every single server in the whole place. Killer taught me a lot about hockey, but even more about respecting people."

Logan's mettle was put to the test a couple times during his draft season of 2006-07. First, even before the season began, he had a setback at Team Canada's training camp for the Ivan Hlinka Tournament, an under-18 event held each summer in the Czech Republic and Slovakia. Logan was set to be one of Canada's go-to forwards before a skate blade cut him close to his knee in the last game before the team was officially selected. After he put that behind him, Logan contracted mononucleosis, which kept him out of the 67's lineup for a portion of time and put him a step behind all year.

Still, Logan averaged nearly 1.5 points per game, notching 78 in just 54 contests. That was enough to convince the Sharks he was for real. San Jose did some wheeling and dealing, pulling the trigger on two draft-day trades, to land Logan ninth overall.

After a couple more seasons with the 67's, Logan made the jump to the pros, splitting time between Worcester and San Jose in 2009-10. The following year, he was ready for primetime. Still officially a rookie, Logan became a vital cog in the Sharks attack, notching 32 goals and 56 points in 79 games.

His output earned him a Calder Trophy nomination and he was just edged out for rookie-of-the-year honors by Carolina Hurricanes sniper Jeff Skinner. Perhaps most impressively, when the Sharks were in unfamiliar territory halfway though the 2010-11 season, floundering outside the playoffs, Logan was one of the driving forces behind a turnaround that saw San Jose capture another Pacific Division title and advance to the Western Conference final for the second consecutive year.

John, his agent, said Logan has absolutely no sense of entitlement and what sets him apart from other good young players is that he's willing to work very hard for everything he wants to achieve. That intensity has been on display forever and Ted said his son's burning competitive instincts surfaced in every scenario, whether he was sitting around the poker table, taking aim at flagsticks on the golf course or having a fierce mini-stick battle with his younger brother, Judson. Logan was also an avid baseball player as a kid and, just like when he was on the ice, nobody on the diamond was going to intimidate him.

"If somebody threw a brush-back pitch at him in a baseball game, he'd just stand in there for the next pitch and wallop it," Ted said. "Just nothing would seem to faze him. Not too many people have that." – *Ryan Dixon*

★★★★★★★★★★★★★★★★★★★★★★★★★★★★★★★★★

**LOGAN COUTURE'S FAVORITE [...]
GROWING UP**

PLAYER: PAT LAFONTAINE
JERSEY: BUFFALO SABRES
CARTOON: RECESS
ALBUM: HOUSE OF BALLOONS BY THE WEEKND
MOVIE: DUMB AND DUMBER
VIDEO GAME: CALL OF DUTY
SPORT OTHER THAN HOCKEY: BASEBALL
SCHOOL SUBJECT: PHYS-ED
JUNK FOOD: LIFESAVER GUMMIES

★★★★★★★★★★★★★★★★★★★★★★★★★★★★★★★★★

STEVEN STAMKOS

TAMPA BAY LIGHTING

POSITION: CENTER
DRAFTED: 1ST OVERALL IN 2008
BORN: FEBRUARY 7, 1990 – MARKHAM, ONT.
LAST DEVELOPMENTAL TEAM: SARNIA STING (OHL)

Some things cannot be taught. You either have it or you don't.

The first time Paul Titanic saw the kid with the oversized Toronto Maple Leafs jersey on the ice, the youth coach knew Steven Stamkos had it. It was like watching a baby bird leave the nest for the first time. The three-year-old could fly. Most kids learn to skate by holding onto chairs and repeatedly falling on their butts. But Steven seemed born for this.

He did crossovers. He sprayed snow when he stopped. He even went backwards.

> "Without exaggeration, Steven could fire the puck under the crossbar at age three."
>
> **– Paul Titanic**

"Without exaggeration, he could fire the puck under the crossbar," said Titanic, who first coached Steven when he was five. "If there was a defender between him and another guy, he could saucer it over. It was just incredible. His skating ability – his edgework – was at a level far, far beyond his years."

It would be like this for a while. Steven, like Wayne Gretzky and Sidney Crosby, was a child prodigy. And not just at hockey. Whether he was kicking a soccer ball or swinging a baseball bat, he had a knack for making the difficult look easy.

In many ways, it was.

STEVEN STAMKOS, WHOSE TRAINING WITH GARY ROBERTS HAS BECOME A HOT TOPIC AROUND THE NHL, ALREADY HAS A ROCKET RICHARD TROPHY ON HIS SHELF AND HEARD HIS NAME BANDIED AROUND WITH CROSBY AND OVECHKIN'S.

"He's an all-around jock," said Steven's father, Chris. "His soccer team won an Ontario championship, his baseball team won an Ontario championship and his lacrosse team won an Ontario championship. So he's won four Ontario championships in four different sports.

"It was always important for him to play different sports. I think when you're younger, the more you can play the better off you're going to be when you decide to focus on one particular sport. Each adds a different element of skill sets. It all helps. Having played baseball, you can sometimes bat the puck out of the air."

No question, Steven is skilled. You have to be to play in the NHL. But the reason why the Tampa Bay Lightning center has become one of the most feared snipers in the NHL is more than just about the abilities he was born with.

Every player has degree of talent. It is what you do with that talent that defines a player's career. And from an early age, Steven seemed to understand what separated the good players from the great ones.

In what was perhaps his first interview, a 10-year-old Steven spoke about the importance of being a team player to the *National Post* for a feature entitled "Seven secrets of highly successful kids." The framed article still hangs on a wall at his parents' house.

"In sports you have to have a good attitude to play the game," he said at the time. "You shouldn't always carry the puck or ball end-to-end – pass it up and move and maybe he'll pass it back to you. Give and go. There are some kids who don't pass the puck or the ball and then you're wide open and they lose it.

"You've gotta tell them, 'Nice try, but next time, he was open, so you could pass it to him and we'll have a better scoring chance.' You have to say good things and then they're confident instead of yelling and thinking they can't do it so they won't try."

Yes, long before he was drafted first overall into the NHL or was even playing in the Ontario League, Steven seemed to have it all figured out.

Pass the puck. Don't yell at your teammates. Be positive.

Of course, these things were easy while playing AAA hockey for the Markham Waxers.

"It was a dynasty team," Steven said.

Among his teammates were future New York Rangers defenseman Michael Del Zotto, Vancouver Canucks center Cody Hodgson and Colorado Avalanche defenseman Cameron Gaunce.

With that much star power, Steven had no problems using his linemates. Nor did Markham have much trouble winning. In Steven's six years playing for the Waxers, they captured two Ontario championships and finished with silver and bronze medals two other times.

"At the time, you know that they're all talented players," said Titanic, who was Markham's coach. "But so much has to happen and so much has to go right for them to sign an NHL contract. But certainly the character of the kids at that time did show they would have a good chance to do it."

One game, in particular, typified what his team – and Steven – was made of. The Waxers were trailing 5-1 with about seven minutes remaining and the other team had started acting a bit cocky. So Titanic called a timeout and told his talented squad that the game was far from over.

"To make a long story short, we ended up winning 6-5 in overtime," Titanic said. "Steven had five goals and an assist in the game. So it was incredible. Basically they couldn't stop him for the last seven minutes of the game. And then in overtime, he actually set up the winning goal. It was an incredible spectacle."

It does not have to be hockey. It can be something as trivial as a pre-game warmup of playing keep-up with a soccer ball or video games. Make a competition out of something and Steven plays to win. In a way, he is borderline obsessive about it.

"You have to know when to take it easy if it's for fun," Steven said. "But when it comes down to crunch time, I hate losing. I think you have to have that mentality to be an elite athlete."

One time, as a member of the OHL's Sarnia Sting, he and the family he was billeting with were battling to see who could hit the furthest home run in a Nintendo Wii baseball game. Andrew Shaw, the father of

> **"When it comes down to crunch time, I hate losing. You have to have that mentality to be an elite athlete."**
>
> **– Steven Stamkos**

the house, blasted a pitch that went 624 feet and trotted around the room as though he was Albert Pujols. Furious, Steven vowed to top it. Five hours later, while Shaw was sleeping, Steven finally did. And for good measure, he knocked on Shaw's door to let him know it.

"It wasn't good enough that he knew he beat me," Shaw said. "He had to wake me up and physically show me."

That desire to be the best is why Steven spends his summers working out with hockey player-turned-fitness guru Gary Roberts, where he is pushed to the point of puking. It is also why he still goes on the ice with a stickhandling expert from Finland to work on his already-impressive hands.

"He has the drive to become better at the things that he's doing, there's no question about it," said Jari Byrski, founder of SK8ON hockey school. "But what also impresses me is he doesn't use the pressure to destroy him."

In his first year in the OHL (2006-07), after being chosen first overall by Sarnia, Steven's 42 goals and 92 points placed him third behind Patrick Kane and Sam Gagner in rookie scoring. Those two played for the same high-powered London Knights team and were a year older – they went first and sixth overall in the 2007 NHL draft.

Steven also became an Internet sensation for a shootout goal scored at that year's OHL all-star game skills competition. It was a move, he said, that was born out of embarrassment.

Moments earlier, Steven had made the blooper reel when he lost an edge and crashed into the end boards during the fastest skater event. As he picked himself up, about 4,000 fans in Saginaw, Mich., were having a rare laugh at his expense.

"I didn't want to be the guy remembered for falling," he said. "We had the breakaway competition right after that and I decided to try it. I had already fallen, so I had nothing to lose. I figured they were already going to remember me as the guy who fell."

No one remembers Steven for falling. Instead, they remember him as the guy who scored a shootout goal with his hands invisibly tied behind his back.

"He came down kind of slow, so I didn't really know what he was going to do," remembered goaltender Andrew Perugini, who was in net for the goal. "He kind of went to the backhand, so I thought he might try to put it high. And as I was sliding over, he put it behind his back and flipped it the other way over my shoulder and it stuck under the bar."

"I guess the hockey gods were looking after me," Steven laughed.

They apparently still are. Not that he needs much in the way of help.

In his first year in the NHL, the learning curve was steep. But midway through the season, Steven finally caught on and ended up finishing with a respectable 23 goals and 46 points.

The following season, he became the third-youngest player to score 50 goals – he finished with 51 goals and 95 points – and tied Crosby for the Rocket Richard Trophy. In his third year, he scored 45 goals and 91 points and then helped the Lightning come within one game of advancing to the Stanley Cup final.

But this is just the beginning for the rising star.

"If you want something bad enough, you can do it," Steven said. "Whether it's something little like beating someone in Wii or making it to the NHL as an 18-year-old. If it's something I want to accomplish and want to do, I'm going to do whatever it takes – within the limits – to get there." – Michael Traikos

★★★★★★★★★★★★★★★★★★★★★★★★★★★★★★★★★

STEVEN STAMKOS' FAVORITE [...] GROWING UP

PLAYER: STEVE YZERMAN
CARTOON: FLINSTONES
MUSICIAN: EMINEM
MOVIE: REMEMBER THE TITANS
VIDEO GAME: EA SPORTS NHL SERIES
SPORT OTHER THAN HOCKEY: BASEBALL
SCHOOL SUBJECTS: GYM AND ENGLISH
JUNK FOOD: KETCHUP CHIPS

★★★★★★★★★★★★★★★★★★★★★★★★★★★★★★★★★

DREW DOUGHTY

LOS ANGELES KINGS

POSITION: DEFENSE

DRAFTED: 2ND OVERALL IN 2008

BORN: DECEMBER 8, 1989 – LONDON, ONT.

LAST DEVELOPMENTAL TEAM: GUELPH STORM (OHL)

Watching Los Angeles Kings defenseman Drew Doughty skate the puck up the ice evokes poetry in motion, so it's weird to think cruising down the ice would have ever given him problems. But when a young Drew suited up for the first time, his feet weren't too co-operative.

"I couldn't skate very well," he said. "There were times when I was discouraged because I sucked so much."

Hard to believe the second overall pick in the 2008 draft would have such grave concerns about his game, but it just goes to prove how players develop at different rates. Fortunately for Drew, he didn't give up on hockey. Maybe the fact he had his sights set on the NHL's biggest star played a role in that determination.

"I was a big Wayne Gretzky fan," he said. "Whenever he was on the east coast, I'd watch him."

But with The Great One based out of Los Angeles at the time, 7:30 starts in Drew's London, Ont., home were a rarity.

"I remember crying, not wanting to go to bed," Drew said. "I wanted to watch the game."

> "I remember crying, not wanting to go to bed. I wanted to watch the game."
>
> **– Drew Doughty**

Thanks in large part to Gretzky, Drew grew up a Kings fan in a place far from 'Tinseltown.' Along with an L.A. Kings phone in his room, he had a Kelly Hrudey jersey and another silver-and-black classic with a twist: No. 99 was the number, but "Doughty" was the name across the shoulders.

Back in those days, Drew was a forward. It wasn't until a training camp in minor bantam that the prospect of defense came up. His team was short of blueliners and his coach asked him if he would make the switch.

"I wasn't very keen on it," Drew said. "But it worked out pretty well. It gave me these hands and the ability to make plays in tight."

Indeed, the smooth-skating youngster made his mark early. In just his second year of major junior hockey with the Ontario League's Guelph Storm, Drew racked up a remarkable 53 assists and 74 points in just 67 games. However, the fact a kid who grew up in the home of the rival London Knights was doing big things for another team became problematic...in a fun way.

"By the end of my junior career in Guelph, the London fans were booing me," he recalled.

With a December birthday, Drew had to wait an extra year before he was eligible for the NHL draft. He made the most of that final year of teen hockey, joining Canada's world junior team in the Czech Republic over the Christmas break. Though he didn't score a goal at the tournament, Drew did tally four assists in seven games. Most importantly, he helped Canada to a fourth straight gold medal thanks to a 3-2 overtime win over Sweden in the final. Drew was named the tournament's top defenseman for his efforts.

"The world juniors was huge for me," he said. "I had never been on that type of stage before. But that helped me a lot. It gave me the confidence to know I could play NHL hockey."

Considering other players at the tournament included Steven Stamkos, James van Riemsdyk and Victor Hedman, Drew was correct in his assessment of the WJC's clout. But there was one aspect of his game that stood in his way and NHL scouts weren't afraid to tell Drew about it. Despite his amazing skating and vision, the Guelph defenseman had to work on his conditioning.

43

DREW DOUGHTY HAS
BEEN A STAR FOR THE
LOS ANGELES KINGS,
BUT FIRST HE HAD TO
PROVE HE WAS
COMMITTED TO
GETTING IN
NHL-CALIBER SHAPE.

"Diet was the biggest part of it," Drew said. "Before I was eating three big meals and crushing appetizers. Now it's six small meals. It changes your metabolism."

The Kings were very interested in Drew and with the second pick in the draft, could surely get him if they wanted his services. Tampa Bay had made it very clear it was going to take Stamkos with the first pick, but that didn't mean Drew could rest on his laurels.

"His talent was never, ever an issue," said Michael Futa, co-director of amateur scouting for the Kings. "He was always a special player. But as it got closer to decision time, our biggest concern was conditioning. We really called him out on it. We visited his house and told him it wouldn't help to do the Atkins diet or throw on a garbage bag to lose a couple pounds right away."

It would have to be a lifestyle choice and Drew committed. He was approximately 230 pounds at the time (and just six feet tall), but worked enough that he had shed 20 pounds by the time the draft combine rolled around in early summer.

"He had obviously taken everything we said seriously," Futa recalled. "I couldn't have been happier."

Particularly since the other aspects of Drew's game were so enticing. Futa saw the slick blueliner play quite a bit in Guelph and also coached him as a member of Canada's under-17 team. He likened the teen's vision to that of NFL quarterback Tom Brady, checking passing options as he skated the puck up the ice. And on a Guelph team that didn't boast a lot of elite talent, Drew was given a lot of ice time – a "criminal amount," Futa joked.

The Kings scouting staff watched video of prospects in isolation and as fun as it was to watch Drew, it was the hockey equivalent of *Lord of the Rings*.

"As a staff member, if you were doing a Drew Doughty game, you better get a coffee because he'd be on the ice 35 minutes," Futa said. "And lord help you if the game went into overtime."

But like the Middle Earth epic, watching Drew was a treat. He could cut through an entire team when he wanted to, but had to learn to pick his spots because his advanced play would sometimes catch teammates off guard.

Getting drafted by the team you grow up idolizing is every kid's dream, but Drew had to sit on pins and needles all the way until the podium. First, there was the fact fellow defenseman Zach Bogosian was quickly stalking him on the draft charts, bringing a physically powerful intense game that was in stark contrast to Drew's easy-going assassin routine. Then on draft day, there was talk of Los Angeles making a trade.

"All I could think was that they got rid of the second pick," Drew said.

But the Kings kept that slot and indeed made Drew their selection. From there, it was straight to the NHL for the 2008-09 campaign. His efforts that first season earned him a place on the NHL's all-rookie team, but it was Drew's sophomore year that truly cemented his place in the hockey world.

On the strength of 16 goals and 59 points in 82 games, Drew was named a second-team all-star and a Norris Trophy-nominee while helping the Kings to their first playoff berth since 2002. He played nearly 25 minutes a game in the process, proving junior was no fluke.

In February of that season, however, Drew really grabbed the spotlight. Team Canada GM Steve Yzerman chose the second-year pro to suit up for the nation's Olympic team in Vancouver, bypassing more established blueliners such as Mike Green and Jay Bouwmeester in the process. As it turned out, Yzerman's instincts proved correct, as Drew thrived on the biggest stage imaginable.

"His first game was a bit of a warmup," Futa said. "By the second or third game, he was the best player in that tournament."

Entering the Games as a depth defenseman, Drew pushed his way to the top, eventually pairing with Chicago's Duncan Keith on Canada's No. 1 unit. The fact Keith's regular partner on the Blackhawks, Brent Seabrook, was also on the squad made

Entering the 2010 Olympic Games as a depth defenseman, Drew Doughty pushed his way to the top, eventually pairing with Chicago's Duncan Keith on Canada's No. 1 unit.

the usurping all the more incredible. And, of course, the tourney ended with Canada grabbing gold over the rival U.S. in an incredible overtime win.

"That was so crazy," Drew said. "We had so much pressure on us. I was so happy to be part of that group and it was a big part of my development."

A development yet to be completed. Despite the early success, Futa said 'Olympic Drew' is the everyday goal in Los Angeles. But he believes Drew will get there.

"I have no question," Futa said, "a guy like that should accidentally be in the All-Star Game every year."

On the ice, Drew has been described as one of the game's best chirpers, even though he knows guys have plenty of fire-back fodder when it comes to his physical frame.

"He's very casual," Futa said. "He's witty, sarcastic – that's what makes Drew, Drew."

A young man who's easy-going off the ice and make things look easy on it. – *Ryan Kennedy*

★★★★★★★★★★★★★★★★★★★★★★★★★★★★★★★★★★

DREW DOUGHTY'S FAVORITE [...] GROWING UP

JERSEY: LOS ANGELES KINGS
CARTOON: ARTHUR
MUSICIAN: EMINEM
VIDEO GAME: EA SPORTS NHL SERIES
SCHOOL SUBJECT: PHYS-ED
JUNK FOOD: CHOCOLATE BARS

★★★★★★★★★★★★★★★★★★★★★★★★★★★★★★★★★★

LUKE SCHENN

TORONTO MAPLE LEAFS

POSITION: DEFENSE
DRAFTED: 5TH OVERALL IN 2008
BORN: NOVEMBER 2, 1989 – SASKATOON, SASK.
LAST DEVELOPMENTAL TEAM: KELOWNA ROCKETS (WHL)

At 6-foot-2 and 229 pounds, size has a lot to do with what Luke Schenn can do on the ice. But if you were to see him as a 10-year-old, you'd guess size had a lot to do with what he couldn't do.

> ## "If you saw pictures of me growing up, I don't think people would believe how fat I actually was."
> ## – Luke Schenn

"If you saw pictures of me growing up, I don't think people would believe how fat I actually was," Luke said with a laugh.

Indeed, true to his Prairie boy roots, Luke has always been beefy. As a kid growing up on hockey-mad Hurley Crescent in Saskatoon, Sask., his girth often helped him thrive in a role he loved from the beginning – shutdown defenseman. While most kids tend to gravitate toward the glory of scoring goals or the cool equipment and day-saving possibilities presented to a goalie, Luke relished being a human blanket, crushing the creative attempts of exuberant youngsters.

"I always loved that," he said.

As for his prosperous proportions, Jeff Schenn, Luke's dad and often his youth hockey coach, said it's not as though the family was feeding Luke any more than the next kid; it's just that he had a tougher time burning it off. Eventually he started to shed the baby fat, but as he came into his teenage years, Luke realized he was going to have to work at getting more fit.

Both Luke and Jeff also point to Luke's heavier frame as an example that making the NHL doesn't happen when you're barely a decade old, a lesson some overzealous parents who have very young kids in rinks year-round might learn from.

"Kids these days, in my opinion, are doing a little too much at a young age for hockey," Luke said.

Added Jeff: "You'll see even these young hockey stars and I know some now in Saskatchewan who are starting to get some summer hockey going on when they're seven and eight years old. People just have to realize that it's a long journey to get where they're going to."

Luke is the oldest of four kids, with brother Brayden two years his junior, followed by sisters Madison and Macy. Brayden, who was drafted fifth overall by the L.A. Kings in 2009 and subsequently dealt to the Philadelphia Flyers, was happy to offer some in-house competition for Luke as the boys were growing up, but he certainly wasn't the only other kid in the neighborhood who knew how to handle a stick. According to Jeff, more than a handful of the youngsters who grew up close by have gone on to join either major junior or the university-level ranks.

When it was just the two of them on the family's backyard rink, the dynamic between the Schenn boys was perfect because Brayden, an offense-minded center, could perfect his dangles against a big brother who was honing his defensive skills.

"That's how it kind of worked out 1-on-1," Luke said. "I'd always want to be the defenseman and he'd always want to be the forward and work on his moves."

Looking back on his youth hockey days, a few events stand out to Luke as seminal moments. Two involve trips to Alberta for famous hockey events, the first being The Brick Invitational Super Novice Tournament, where Luke was a young member of the Saskatchewan Hustlin' Huskies. Several years later, Luke was headed west again to participate in the prestigious Mac's AAA Midget Tournament in Calgary.

Both events attract players and teams from all over North America and, especially as a midget player, it was an eye-opener for Luke to see how he fared against some of the top talent in his age group.

49

THE LEAFS MOVED UP THE 2008 DRAFT TO GRAB ONE OF THE TWO FAMOUS SCHENN BROS. IT'S SURELY GOING TO BE A TENSE NIGHT WHEN THE TWO FINALLY FACE OFF ON NHL ICE.

"You're just some kid from Saskatoon," he said. "You don't really know if you stand a chance for real."

Luke's midget team, the Saskatoon Contacts, won the national title at the 2005 Telus Cup in Gatineau, Que. According to Jeff, Luke wasn't really a top-four defenseman on that club, but he was about to get up close and personal with one of the best junior-aged blueliners in the world. The Western League's Kelowna Rockets, who had made Luke their top pick in the 2004 WHL Bantam Draft, were one of the four teams competing for the 2005 Memorial Cup in London, Ont.

The tournament had an added dose of excitement for a number of reasons: the inclusion of wunderkind Sidney Crosby and his Rimouski Oceanic, the fact the hometown Knights were one of the best junior outfits ever and the absence of a Stanley Cup final that year due to the NHL lockout. Luke was asked to come along, not to compete, but simply for the experience of soaking it all in and seeing the highest version of the next level up close and personal.

And even with all that was going on at the tourney, perhaps the best part for Luke was the fact he had a chance to keep close company with the Rockets captain.

"I got to room with Shea Weber, so that was a pretty cool experience for me," he said. "I got to know him pretty well."

While the hockey world was watching Corey Perry and the Knights beat Crosby and the Oceanic for the Memorial Cup title, Luke was learning what it would take to be a contributor the next year in Kelowna.

"I knew I needed to get in way better shape to play at that level," he said.

Even with his heightened focus, there were no guarantees Luke would get a lot of playing time when he headed to Kelowna for the 2005-06 season. The team lost Weber, but still featured older standouts like future NHLers Alex Edler, now of the Vancouver Canucks, and Kyle Cumiskey of the Colorado Avalanche. In fact, Jeff, who knew Rockets GM-owner Bruce Hamilton, respectfully asked that if Luke wasn't going to see the ice much, he be returned to Saskatoon so he could play more at home.

But that wasn't going to be an issue. By Christmas of that season, Luke had burrowed his way into the team's top four. Then, as Edler and Cumiskey moved on from their junior careers, Luke was leaned on even more heavily.

"They gave him a lot more responsibility and he kind of took it and ran with it," Jeff said.

By his third WHL season, Luke was a force. During the holiday season that year, he travelled to the Czech Republic as part of Canada's entry at the 2008 World Junior Championship. Luke finished the tourney with a team-best plus-5 rating as Canada won gold.

At the NHL draft in 2008, the Toronto Maple Leafs traded up to nab Luke with the fifth overall pick, the team's highest selection since taking Scott Thornton third overall in 1989, the year Luke was born.

By setting the bar where he did, Ron Wilson tapped into Luke Schenn's competitive and determined nature.

By the time Leafs camp rolled around in September of '08, Luke was already feeling the intense scrutiny that comes with being a part of Canada's most-watched hockey club after he turned in a poor showing at a rookie tournament in Kitchener, Ont.

"I remember being pretty bad at that tournament and I was taking a lot of heat for it already from fans," he said.

By the time camp rolled around, Luke, still a couple months shy of his 19th birthday, sat about 10th on the organizational depth chart among defensemen. Making the task of cracking the team even tougher was the fact new Toronto bench boss Ron Wilson had set a high standard for Luke to clear if he was going to make the jump to the big show. By setting the bar where he did, Wilson tapped into Luke's competitive and determined nature.

"I remember turning the TV on one day when I was in the hotel," Luke said. "Ron Wilson was on saying 'the only way we're going to keep him is if he can show us he can play on our top four, otherwise we're going to send him back.' Kelowna is a great place to play, but I wanted to make the NHL right then and there."

With the parameters clearly set, Luke went out and earned a spot on the team with his no-nonsense approach and ability to clear the puck from danger zones. Validating Toronto's decision to keep him was the fact Luke made the NHL's 2009 all-rookie team alongside Los Angeles Kings star Drew Doughty on the blueline. During his time wearing the Blue & White, Luke has become a respected leader and a hard-rock defenseman, topping all players at his position with 251 hits in 2010-11.

That pudgy kid from Saskatoon who once wondered if he belonged with the best has become a punisher. And the only question left to answer now is, just how good can Hurley Crescent's most tenacious defender be? – *Ryan Dixon*

★★★★★★★★★★★★★★★★★★★★★★★★★★★★★★★★★★★

LUKE SCHENN'S FAVORITE [...] GROWING UP

PLAYER: ROB BLAKE
JERSEY: TORONTO MAPLE LEAFS
MEMORABILIA: SIGNED KEITH TKACHUK STICK
CARTOON: THE SIMPSONS
MUSICIAN: GARTH BROOKS
MOVIE: HAPPY GILMORE
VIDEO GAME: EA SPORTS NHL SERIES
SPORT OTHER THAN HOCKEY: GOLF
SUBJECT: PHYS-ED
JUNK FOODS: ICE CREAM AND POTATO CHIPS

★★★★★★★★★★★★★★★★★★★★★★★★★★★★★★★★★★★

TYLER MYERS

BUFFALO SABRES

POSITION: DEFENSE
DRAFTED: 12TH OVERALL IN 2008
BORN: FEBRUARY 1, 1990 – HOUSTON, TEXAS
LAST DEVELOPMENTAL TEAM: KELOWNA ROCKETS (WHL)

At 6-foot-8, it's pretty easy to make a joke about Tyler Myers having the frame of a basketball player, not an NHLer. But based on where he grew up, it's actually not much of a stretch.

The Buffalo Sabres defenseman spent his early years in Houston, Texas, where hockey is far from the No. 1 sport.

"Growing up, hockey was certainly not my first sport," he said. "I played basketball, baseball and soccer. I was always good at basketball, given my height."

But Tyler's dad, Paul, played hockey in college and came from northern roots (Paul's dad came from Boston). When Tyler was six years old, his father took him to a Houston Aeros game, back when the team was part of the International League. The impact was immediate.

"We started buying equipment the next day," Tyler said.

But in Houston, minor hockey wasn't as organized as it would have been even in Dallas, which had the benefit of the NHL's Stars and the grassroots movement that came along with them. But Paul would play street hockey with Tyler in the driveway and go that extra mile to get him on ice, despite the difficulties.

"Down there it's a challenge," Paul said. "It's a long drive to the arenas and there's no one to play."

There was also the matter of Tyler's skills at the time.

"It was his favorite sport," Paul said, "but the one he was worst at."

That would soon change, however. Paul had originally come to Houston by way of New Orleans. In both cities he worked for Amoco, an oil company, as a geophysicist.

But his roots were pulling him north and, based on his career at the time, the choices were Denver or Calgary. In 2000, 10-year-old Tyler moved to Alberta with his father and step-mom.

Now in a hotbed of hockey, there were no struggles for Tyler to find competition and the rinks were much easier to get to. But where would he fit in?

When tryouts came, kids were separated into 13 groups based on how skilled the coaches thought they were. Tyler started out right in the middle – Team 7 – but kept getting bumped up.

"I think he spent five hours on the ice that day," Paul said. "By the end he was on Team 1."

So began Tyler's ascent in hockey. And so, too, began his physical ascent. By Grade 8, Tyler was six-feet tall. He had a big growth spurt around age 14, bringing him up to 6-foot-3. At 15 he was 6-foot-5 and finally rose to 6-foot-8 by the time he was 18. Having so many jumps came with drawbacks, particularly in hockey where balance and knowing your body is so important.

"It was a challenge for me right through my junior days in Kelowna," Tyler said. "I had to deal with growth spurts that made me feel like I couldn't skate."

Essentially he was re-learning what he was physically capable of every couple years. But Tyler's skills could not be denied. As a teen, he played minor hockey at The Edge School, a private team that often warred with the public system. With uncertainty around the program's place in Calgary, the decision was made for Tyler to take his game to Saskatchewan and the Notre Dame Hounds, a prep school team at Athol Murray College whose alumni include

> **"My height was a challenge for me right through my junior days in Kelowna. I had to deal with growth spurts that made me feel like I couldn't skate."**
>
> **– Tyler Myers**

GROWING UP IN TEXAS, TYLER MYERS WAS EXPOSED TO A NUMBER OF DIFFERENT SPORTS, BUT A MOVE TO CALGARY REALLY HELPED OUT THE FUTURE BUFFALO BLUELINER.

Brad Richards, Rod Brind'Amour and Wendel Clark. Located in tiny Wilcox, it was definitely a change of pace for Tyler.

"It was different, for sure," he said. "The school has more students than the town itself has people."

But Tyler loved the dorm room atmosphere and three of his friends from Calgary came with him, so that took some of the homesickness away. Fellow Hounds that year included Anaheim's Brandon McMillan and Toronto's Joe Colborne.

Tyler's next stop was Kelowna, B.C., where he suited up for the Western League's Rockets. Although his first full campaign was a struggle for the team, each successive season got better and in 2009 the Rockets won the WHL championship and played for the Memorial Cup, losing to Windsor and Taylor Hall in the final. But Tyler still had to prove to some folks that he had legitimate greatness inside him.

"There were a lot of doubters, especially in junior when I was still growing into my body," he said. "But I'm not the type of person to get worked up over things. There are a lot of people who love you and a lot of people who hate you."

Throughout it all, Tyler knew his father had his back and credits him for pushing the young defenseman when he needed it. Paul says he realized Tyler might be a truly special talent when the son was 16 years old in Kelowna.

"He was a good player, but there were a lot of holes," Paul said. "But I saw glimpses when he had full energy. Then it was just a matter of him filling in his body."

By his NHL draft year in 2008, Tyler weighed 204 pounds. He has since put on another 23 pounds and if his early pro career is any indication, all those growing pains were worth it.

Taken 12th overall by the Sabres in 2008, Tyler was regarded as a high-risk, high-reward pick at the time. Playing for a well-regarded junior team certainly bolstered his stock, but there were still ups and downs.

"It was pretty stressful going up to the draft," Paul said. "You want him to reach his dreams. He has a bad game with Kelowna and you feel it."

Returning to the WHL after being drafted to further develop his game, Tyler was excellent for Canada's world junior team, pairing with future Toronto Maple Leaf Keith Aulie (himself a behemoth at 6-foot-5) to help his country win gold in Ottawa. That was also the year he helped Kelowna to the Memorial Cup alongside future NHLers Jamie Benn and his old friend Brandon McMillan.

The next year, Tyler was a revelation for the Buffalo Sabres as a rookie, demonstrating a smooth-skating stride and terrific skills with the puck. He played in all 82 games, notching 11 goals and 48 points, placing him third among all rookies behind only John Tavares and Matt Duchene. He averaged an impressive 23:44 of ice time per game, tops among rookies, while his plus-13 placed him second. In a year where he wasn't the biggest name to start off, Tyler was awarded the Calder Trophy as the NHL's rookie of the year and there really wasn't much of a question he would win. For the lanky rearguard, determination was the key.

"Having the mindset of never being satisfied and always wanting more helped me win the Calder," he said.

"It's wrong of me to admit, but I was a Dallas Stars fan when they beat the Sabres in 1999."

– Tyler Myers

Tyler is now a cornerstone of the Buffalo franchise. But there is one part of his Texas history that might make longtime Buffalo fans cringe just a little.

"It's wrong of me to admit," he said, "but I was a Dallas Stars fan when they beat the Sabres in 1999."

That was the closest Buffalo has come to winning the Stanley Cup so far, but it'd be hard not to forgive a nine-year-old kid for cheering on the nearest NHL team.

In those early days, Tyler actually played forward and listed Steve Yzerman of the Red Wings and Dallas' own Mike Modano as his heroes.

Tyler's own potential is still developing, but his father has a lot of faith in him, even if Tyler sometimes needs to be hounded before he gets on track.

"We always joked that Tyler does things on 'Tyler time,'" Paul said.

In his second NHL season, Tyler began the year with a bit of a sophomore slump. Some attributed it to the loss of defense partner Henrik Tallinder, who had left via free agency for

New Jersey, while others pointed to the fact it appeared the youngster was simply trying to do too much on the ice. By the end of the season he had righted the ship and, in fact, was a big offensive contributor in the playoffs, tallying six points in a seven-game loss to the Philadelphia Flyers. Now he's looking ahead to future success.

"I would love to be the go-to guy," he said. "It's going to take a lot of consistency and hard work, but I feel I've made huge strides in my game."

If anyone can accurately talk about huge strides, it's Tyler. But along with his play for the Sabres, his father has other reasons to be impressed with him.

"I'm proud of him in many aspects outside of hockey," Paul said. "I see him talking to kids after practices. He remembers where he came from; he's got a good heart."
– *Ryan Kennedy*

★★★★★★★★★★★★★★★★★★★★★★★★★★★★★★★★★

TYLER MYERS' FAVORITE [...] GROWING UP

JERSEY: DETROIT RED WINGS
MEMORABILIA: SIGNED PHOTOS OF BOBBY ORR AND NICK LIDSTROM
CARTOON: SCOOBY-DOO
MUSICIAN: JOURNEY
MOVIE: FORREST GUMP
VIDEO GAME: MARIO KART
SPORT OTHER THAN HOCKEY: BASKETBALL
SCHOOL SUBJECT: PHYS-ED
JUNK FOOD: FRUIT ROLL-UPS

★★★★★★★★★★★★★★★★★★★★★★★★★★★★★★★★★

JEFF SKINNER

CAROLINA HURRICANES

POSITION: CENTER

DRAFTED: 7TH OVERALL IN 2010

BORN: MAY 16, 1992 – TORONTO, ONT.

LAST DEVELOPMENTAL TEAM: KITCHENER RANGERS (OHL)

Carolina Hurricanes star Jeff Skinner is very comfortable in his skates and he should be – up until he became a teenager, Jeff was also one of the best figure skaters in his age group for Ontario. Coming from a family in which all six children were figure skaters, Jeff separated himself from his siblings.

"Jeff was different," said Andrew Skinner, his father. "He skated at a much higher competitive level."

This is saying something, because the Skinner kids – two boys and four girls – also had some pretty good hockey players in their ranks. Older brother Ben even shared a dressing room with Jeff when both were members of the Ontario League's Kitchener Rangers for a season. But Jeff's preternatural ability on blades was obvious from the start.

"The first time he was on skates he was probably two and a half," Andrew said. "He was striding right away. It was as if he had a low center of gravity; he could go end to end."

Jeff's first hockey memories come a little later and skew more to the funnier aspect of house league.

"I remember playing goalie when I was four or five – I started playing when I was three," Jeff said. "We would rotate playing goalie. I used to get bored and skate around and I'd get yelled at by the coach because the puck would be coming down to my end and I'd be off in the corner."

Fortunately, Jeff's proclivity for putting pucks in the net, rather than keeping them out, would eventually be his ticket to the big time. But in those early days, figure skating was also a huge part of his life.

"My mom was in it and my older sisters had all these trophies that they had won," he said. "I wanted to win those."

Jeff took up figure skating at age six and continued on until he turned 13. He was one of the top-ranked skaters in the province, winning a bronze medal at the 2004 Skate Canada Junior Nationals, but a twist of fate steered his attention onto hockey full-time.

"The truth of it is," Andrew recalled, "he had a minor injury during summer hockey camp, where he bruised his growth plate."

Doctors told Jeff to stay away from practicing figure skating jumps, because of the stress pulling off double axels or triple jumps would have on his body.

"He was off his figure skates and told to avoid jumps for 10 weeks," Andrew said. "That was a turning point. Once he had that break from competition, it was hard to get back into it."

> **"My mom was in figure skating and my older sisters had all these trophies that they had won. I wanted to win those."**
>
> **— Jeff Skinner**

But there was no such problem in hockey and Jeff continued his ascent through the minor ranks. He was always one of the best players for his age, even if he wasn't the biggest kid. He also had some pretty big inspirations in his older twin sisters, Jennifer (who played for Harvard) and Andrea (Cornell).

"They were great role models for me growing up," Jeff said. "I remember going to their games and seeing how cool it was to play in front of those crowds. It left a good impression. The success they had was inspiring for me, seeing their work ethic and where it got them."

Jeff would soon be on a similar trajectory. Following in the footsteps of brother Ben, Jeff came to Kitchener for the 2008-09 season. The Rangers were in rebuild mode, but Jeff still showed tremendous promise by tallying 27 goals and 51 points in 63 games. He stayed with the same billet family as his brother and his parents would make the trek down from Markham for Friday night home games (the trip is about an hour and 20 minutes one-way), easing the transition.

The next season, Ben went on to Wilfred Laurier University in nearby Waterloo, but it was Jeff who took everyone to school. In a breakout performance, he rang up 50 goals and 90 points in 64 games before a stunning playoff run that featured 20 tallies in 20 appearances. The timing was great; Jeff was up for the NHL draft that year, but scouts varied greatly in where he ranked.

In The Hockey News 2010 Draft Preview, he was slotted at No. 25, though a scout's take in the issue foretold him going much higher. That statement would prove prophetic as Carolina stole Jeff with the seventh pick overall.

"I knew Carolina liked me," Jeff said. "I met a bunch of teams picking in the top-12 and I had a feeling I would go around there."

The X factor of the whole decision was that Carolina knew Jeff had been training with Gary Roberts in the summer, who had just helped Tampa Bay's Steven Stamkos rocket from a so-so rookie campaign to a share of the Rocket Richard Trophy with Sidney Crosby one year later. Could Jeff have a similar trajectory?

The Kitchener Rangers star had actually been training with Lorne Goldenberg, Roberts' own training guru, for two summers before that, so he knew the routine.

"I was doing the same exercises and the same workout," Jeff said. "It was about working smart. A lot of guys may get caught up in lifting too heavy and I think that's where you can get in trouble with injuries."

Jeff's dad remembers his youngest son, who was never a huge kid growing up, being on the late end of development, but that had sorted itself out by junior. By the time Carolina drafted him, he came in at 5-foot-10 and 193 pounds.

At the Hurricanes' summer rookie camp he impressed everyone with his strength on the ice and by the time Carolina had to make the tough decisions in the fall, it was Jeff earning his NHL jersey ahead of several other prospects who had been with the organization for longer.

What followed was the thing of NHL dreams. The Hurricanes began the year in Europe, playing their first two regular season games in Helsinki, Finland, against the Minnesota Wild. Carolina won the first match and in Game 2 Jeff made his mark in another victory.

HAVING ONE FOOT IN THE WORLD OF FIGURE SKATING AS HE GREW UP GAVE CAROLINA'S JEFF SKINNER A CHANCE TO EXCEL IN TWO SPORTS.

The rookie got his first NHL point, assisting on a Tuomo Ruutu goal, then sealed the deal by winning the game for Carolina in the shootout. The Skinner clan watched that game from home and Jeff's ascension was really becoming clear.

"The game came back on from a commercial break," Andrew said. "And the full TV screen was filled with Jeff's face as the first shooter in the shootout. We all let out some sort of noise over that."

From there it was a magical campaign for Jeff. He notched 15 points in his first 15 games and kept the offense going. In January, he was named the NHL's rookie of the month and that was probably the second-most exciting part of the new year.

Around the same time, Jeff was tabbed to play in the NHL All-Star Game – not as a rookie who would only participate in the skills competition, but as a full-fledged player in the real game. With the contest being hosted by Carolina, Jeff's local fame skyrocketed to teen idol proportions – which was accurate, since he was still a teenager.

"It was a crazy weekend," Jeff said. "The hometown fans were great. I thought it was amazing. I'm going to remember it for a long time."

On the road, Jeff roomed with two other young Canes; first with defenseman Jamie McBain, then with fellow forward Drayson Bowman. Back in Carolina, he shared an apartment with young backup goalie Justin Peters. That the Hurricanes didn't think Jeff needed a veteran shadowing him all the time speaks volumes about his maturity.

"He's reserved," Andrew said. "He's a good listener and he thinks before he speaks. He's a nice person."

Once Jeff straps on the skates, however, a different person takes over and that Jeff Skinner is a man of action.

> "On the ice, Jeff is extraordinarily competitive and driven. He tried to do the best he can in anything, whether it's sports or school."
>
> — **Andrew Skinner**

"On the ice, he's extraordinarily competitive and driven," Andrew added. "He tried to do the best he can in anything, whether it's sports or school."

Right now, Jeff is best known for sports and with Carolina just missing out on the playoffs in his first season, there is still work to do. But on an individual basis, Jeff couldn't have done much more. He ended the year with 31 goals and 63 points, playing in all 82 games and leading the NHL in points by a rookie. He also decided three games via the shootout.

The cherry on top, of course, was the Calder Trophy for rookie of the year – an award you can only win once in the NHL. Jeff faced stiff competition from San Jose's Logan Couture and Michael Grabner of the New York Islanders, but in the end there was no denying the kid from Carolina.

For a kid who coveted his family's figure skating trophies as a boy, Jeff already has some pretty impressive hardware of his own. – *Ryan Kennedy*

★★★★★★★★★★★★★★★★★★★★★★★★★★★★★★★★★★★

JEFF SKINNER'S FAVORITE [...] GROWING UP

JERSEY: TORONTO MAPLE LEAFS
MEMORABILIA: PITTSBURGH PENGUINS JERSEY SIGNED BY SIDNEY CROSBY
CARTOON: MIGHTY MORPHIN POWER RANGERS
MOVIE: 300
VIDEO GAME: EA SPORTS NHL SERIES
JUNK FOOD: ICE CREAM

★★★★★★★★★★★★★★★★★★★★★★★★★★★★★★★★★★★

JAMES REIMER

TORONTO MAPLE LEAFS

POSITION: GOALIE
DRAFTED: 99TH OVERALL IN 2006
BORN: MARCH 15, 1988 – MORWEENA, MAN.
LAST DEVELOPMENTAL TEAM: RED DEER REBELS (WHL)

If Ray Petkau had been in the dressing room, he would have seen the fresh-faced kid suiting up to play goal and known the guy who was about to guard the crease for his taped-together hockey team was barely a teenager.

But he wasn't in the room, because half an hour earlier, Petkau wasn't planning on playing hockey. A Winnipeg-based player agent, he had the weekend off and only found his way to the rink after a buddy had called and said the team he was entering in a church tournament needed a few more bodies.

If Petkau was a little late, James Reimer was early.

The tournament was for adults, but a dearth of keepers meant an exception would be made for James, just 13 at the time. Petkau's team was already on the ice when he was getting suited up, but upon landing on the bench he quickly noticed this raw-but-talented goalie making a lot of big saves for an overmatched team.

"When he took his mask off I saw that he was maybe only 13 or 14, but the way he played I thought he was a 16- or 17-year-old," Petkau said.

Petkau, who had become an agent about two years prior after spending some time as a Western League scout, quickly started asking some questions about just who this kid was and discovered James had only been playing organized hockey for about a year at that point. That information piqued the agent's interest even more. It also explained why James' technique was undeveloped. But

Petkau saw evidence of innate skill you don't come across every day.

"He had that sixth sense for knowing where the puck was when he lost it in scrambles," Petkau said. "His athleticism at that age was incredible."

By the end of the day, Petkau knew he had to get the full story. He met the Reimers, Marlene and Harold, and learned the family was a very humble, hard-working lot. James grew up the youngest of four kids in tiny Morweena, Man., about 150 kilometers north of Winnipeg. He played sports of all kinds and especially loved strapping on the pads so his brother Mark, three-and-a-half years his senior, could fire shots at him on the road or pond.

But despite James' constant pleas, the Reimers weren't convinced organized hockey was the best place for their son. Raising four children means constant action and driving all over the countryside to arenas would be a huge commitment. Additionally, they weren't necessarily sure dressing room culture jived with the family's deep-rooted Christian values and sensibilities.

But Petkau wasn't the first person to spot James' potential and soon some of the locals were inquiring about whether there was any chance he would be joining a team.

"People were telling us he's really good, he should be playing," Marlene said.

The tipping point occurred when James was 12 years old and the nearby town of Arborg needed a puckstopper.

"We hesitated a bit, but they were persistent and James begged and begged," Marlene said. "He'd been wanting to play for a while."

With that, James' journey to the NHL officially began. Along the way, another good break facilitated being drafted by the Western League's Red Deer Rebels. At the time, Carter Sears

> "When he took his mask off I saw that James was maybe only 13 or 14, but the way he played I thought he was a 16- or 17 year-old. His athleticism at that age was incredible."
>
> **– Ray Petkau**

was the director of player personnel for the Rebels and he decided the team should draft James on the basis of seeing him play one game – a blowout loss, at that.

"It was kind of a hope and a prayer that I got scouted," James said. "The guy had never heard about me, never seen me play. He saw me play one game and drafted me off that game."

But James wasn't exactly on the next bus to Alberta. Marlene and Harold still had reservations about sending their young son, who'd grown up in a Mennonite farming community and attended a very small school, out into the big, crazy world.

"He came from a fairly sheltered life, so we thought that at 16 to kind of just throw him out there wasn't going to be terribly profitable for him," Marlene said.

Only after the family spoke with then-Red Deer coach Brent Sutter and provided their preferences about where James would billet and go to school did the Reimers feel secure letting James leave.

In Red Deer, James held his own for some less-than-stellar Rebels teams and soaked in a lot about how to play the position from goalie coach Andy Nowicki. His late start in organized hockey meant James hadn't really received a lot of specific training in terms of honing his craft. Instead, he just applied what he saw.

"I didn't really have a goalie coach growing up, everything I learned was mostly from watching TV and watching *Hockey Night in Canada*," he said.

While James' skill set had already stood out to a few people who'd seen him play, a couple things conspired to keep him a bit under the radar. One season, he was the last cut from Team West for the World Under-17 Challenge and then a broken thumb prevented him from participating in the World Under-18 Championship.

But the Toronto Maple Leafs still saw enough potential to take him with the 99th pick of the 2006 draft. The road didn't get any smoother just because he was drafted, however.

After three years with Red Deer, James started his pro career in the ECHL, where his playoff-MVP performance guided the South Carolina Stingrays to a Kelly Cup

HUMBLE AND HARD-WORKING, JAMES REIMER HAS BURST FROM RELATIVE OBSCURITY TO BECOME THE SAVIOR IN TORONTO. NOW THE KEY WILL BE KEEPING IT UP FOR MANY YEARS.

championship in 2009. The next year, he played 26 games for the American League's Toronto Marlies and still wasn't the clear No. 1 by the time the 2010-11 AHL season began.

James posted decent numbers with the Marlies to start the year and his big break came on the first day of 2011, when he got his initial NHL start after Leafs No. 1 Jean-Sebastien Giguere was sidelined with a groin injury. Toronto hammered Ottawa 5-1 on New Year's Day and James went on to win four of his first six starts.

His play helped the Leafs gain a few more points, but the team was still buried in the Eastern Conference standings when the NHL went on hiatus for the 2011 All-Star Game. When play resumed after the break, James and the Leafs went on a tear. Though the club ultimately had too much ground to make up in the playoff race, the Leafs responded to Reimer's outstanding positional play.

> ## "There's nothing I hate more than losing."
> ## – James Reimer

Seemingly overnight, the "aw, shucks" kid from Morweena was suddenly excelling at the most pressure-packed position in hockey, while wearing the uniform of the most-watched team in the league. But if you bumped into him on the street, he'd still seem like the same, humble person who worked so hard to make the big show.

"You would never know it's James Reimer, the goalie of the Toronto Maple Leafs just by meeting the guy," said teammate Luke Schenn.

It's important to note that while Reimer does have an easygoing and polite personality, his internal fire burns as hot as anyone's out there.

"He wants to be one of the best and he obviously gets mad when he doesn't play well," Schenn said. "The thing I like about him is he's good throughout the whole day, then all of a sudden you get him to the rink before the game and no one is really talking to him. He's a pretty focused guy and in the zone and he's got a great mental focus before the game."

James himself admits: "There's nothing I hate more than losing."

In addition to his competitive spirit, James has an attention to detail that serves him well. Marlene saw hard evidence of it when James was in high school, where he carried a very impressive average of 93 percent one year.

"It wasn't because he was so exceptionally brilliant, it's because it irked him to have mistakes," Marlene said. "If he had a mistake, he had to figure it out – especially if he had one mistake. If he had half-a-dozen, he'd say, 'You know what, I didn't quite get the material. But if I have one mistake, there's something wrong.' He's a perfectionist in that sense."

After James' breakout with the Leafs, he was rewarded with a three-year contract, which helped him buy a house just outside the downtown core in Toronto with his wife, April.

There are a ton of eyes fixated on him now, as Leafs fans hope they've found their goaltending savior. Petkau believes the kid he spotted that day at a church tournament has the internal determination and the work ethic to thrive in a pressure-cooker.

"He's a great silent leader," Petkau said. "And you don't see that very often from a young guy like that." – *Ryan Dixon*

★★★★★★★★★★★★★★★★★★★★★★★★★★★★★★★★★★

JAMES REIMER'S FAVORITE [...] GROWING UP

PLAYERS: ED BELFOUR AND MARIO LEMIEUX
CARTOON: BUGS BUNNY
VIDEO GAME: BRETT HULL HOCKEY
SPORTS OTHER THAN HOCKEY: SOCCER AND SWIMMING
SCHOOL SUBJECT: SOCIAL STUDIES

★★★★★★★★★★★★★★★★★★★★★★★★★★★★★★★★★★

MATT DUCHENE

COLORADO AVALANCHE

POSITION: CENTER
DRAFTED: 3RD OVERALL IN 2009
BORN: JANUARY 16, 1991 – HALIBURTON, ONT.
LAST DEVELOPMENTAL TEAM: BRAMPTON BATTALION (OHL)

Knowing the guy behind the bench has its privileges. When Colorado Avalanche center Matt Duchene was just a tyke, his family made Christmas-time treks south from their home in Haliburton, Ont., located about three hours north of Toronto, to upstate New York, where uncle Newell Brown was coaching the American League's Adirondack Red Wings.

"We would always have to get an aisle seat at the top of the rink so he could play on the concourse," said Vince Duchene, Matt's father. "He would have his mini-stick with him and would mimic everything on the ice. If they took a faceoff, he took a faceoff."

Once Matt started skating, he even got on the ice with the Adirondack team and that's where hockey history started.

"Chris Osgood played for them at the time and I used to shoot on him," Matt recalled. "Then I scored my first NHL goal against him, so that was cool."

Matt first attended Adirondack games as a two-year-old and his interest in hockey basically started when he could walk. He began skating at three and was playing hockey at four. On top of having Brown on his mom's side of the family, Matt had NHL genes on his dad's side, too, as long time Bruins and Sabres center Andre Savard is Vince's second cousin. So it came as no surprise that Matt tended to dominate when he played against kids his own age.

Because Haliburton is a small town with a limited pool of players, six-year-old Matt was playing against nine- and 10-year-olds and still cruising. That's when Matt and his family faced a big decision about his future. The nearest elite program was an hour and a half south in Lindsay, Ont. Matt would be leaving behind a team full of friends in Haliburton, but he would also be challenged for the first time. Originally, Vince had just been looking for a summer hockey team for his son, but a miscommunication resulted in Matt enrolling on the winter squad. The tough choice had been made for him.

"He was the kind of kid who always wanted to be No. 1," Vince said. "The AAA circuit gave him a bar to reach for."

He would still be a year younger than many of the players in the league, including Steven Stamkos and future teammate Cody Hodgson.

"A full year at that age is a lot different then than it is now," Matt said. "I was always trying to be on their level."

In his last season before entering major junior, Matt posted 69 goals and 106 points in 52 games for the Central Ontario Wolves. That summer, the Ontario League's Brampton Battalion selected him fifth overall, one year after taking Hodgson in the first round.

Matt was heading to the big-time, but the journey had bumps along the way. He had to move from a cottage country atmosphere in Haliburton (population approximately 16,000) to a major suburb of Toronto. Brampton houses more than 510,000 people and more than 110,000 are of East Indian heritage. High school was very different than it had been in Haliburton.

"The first day of school I remember the teacher reading attendance and me not knowing any of the names being called," Matt said. "That's something I'll never forget. It was a huge adjustment."

But Matt had a great billet family that helped him along the way and after an amazing performance at the world under-17 challenge in January – where he led Team Ontario

> **"Matt would have his mini-stick with him and would mimic everything on the ice. If they took a faceoff, he took a faceoff."**
>
> **– Vince Duchene**

MATT DUCHENE HAD TO MAKE A TOUGH DECISION WHEN HE WAS YOUNGER. COMING FROM A SMALL TOWN, HE LEFT HIS HOMETOWN TEAM TO PLAY ON A MORE COMPETITIVE SQUAD FARTHER AWAY.

in scoring and to a gold medal – he began to settle in. It was particularly helpful that Hodgson, a former teammate on summer hockey squads, was already a leader in Brampton.

"He never fell into the whole 'I'm the vet, you're the rookie' thing," Matt said. "I knew I could go to him and pick his brain. I always looked to him to see how he handled situations."

Hodgson's imprint obviously worked. Matt was great in Brampton, helping the Battalion all the way to the OHL final in 2009, tallying 26 points in 21 playoff games. Unfortunately, the Battalion weren't at full strength and ran into the buzz saw known as Taylor Hall's Windsor Spitfires.

"It's too bad we were injured," Matt said. "I think we could have taken it to seven games or even stole the series."

The silver lining in the defeat was that the long playoff run refocused Matt on a goal he had given up on – going first overall in the NHL draft. The long logic had always been that John Tavares would be the top pick in 2009, but Matt wouldn't let that idea kill his motivation.

"After I got cut from the world junior team (he was slowed by injury), I thought it wouldn't happen," Matt said. "So I let that dream go for awhile. But I had a good second half and a pretty decent playoff. Right around the draft it got insane."

That's because Matt wasn't the only one who believed in his elite potential. Pundits began poking holes in Tavares' game and all of a sudden it was a three-horse race with Matt and Swedish defenseman Victor Hedman.

"The morning of the draft, we knew there were three teams and we were going to one of them," Matt said. "But they were three totally different organizations."

The Islanders were choosing first and desperately needed a face for the franchise, preferably one who could score in vast quantities. Tampa held the second selection and with Stamkos, Vincent Lecavalier and Martin St-Louis already in the fold, needed to beef up on defense. Colorado was coming off its worst season ever in Denver and needed fresh blood.

In a neat little twist of fate, Matt had grown up as a fan of the Avalanche. His favorite players were Joe Sakic and Peter Forsberg and uncle Newell even got Sakic to autograph a Colorado sweater for his nephew back in the day. It still hangs in the Duchene family basement.

Sure enough, Matt went to the Avs with the third overall pick while Tavares – his roommate at the draft – was taken first by New York.

"I remember coming back to the room and John had his Isles sweater on and I had my Avs gear on," Matt said. "Things truly did work out for the best. And I grew up an Avalanche fan...what kid doesn't want to play for their favorite team?"

Of course, parents tend to see things from a different light.

> ## "I wouldn't say I'm a tree hugger, but I do love the outdoors."
> # – Matt Duchene

"From the time the season was over until the draft, that was stressful," Vince said. "He flew to Long Island, then Tampa...as a parent, it's not about visiting an NHL team, it's your kid going to a place without you."

When Matt was in Brampton, his folks would drive down to see him play, even though it was a couple hours each way in the car. Vince estimates he only missed one home game in Matt's two years with the Battalion and travelled to Peterborough, Belleville and even Kitchener, too. For a father and son who spent a lot of time in the car during those days in Lindsay, it was par for the course.

But Colorado is not a quick trip from Haliburton.

"When you're in the car with your kid for nine years and you have that personal time, it's like losing your right arm," Vince said. "It was like losing my buddy."

Having time away from the rink has always been important for Matt and his dad, which is why fishing has always played a big role in their relationship. The two have been angling together since Matt was four years old and the first rule of fishing was that there was no hockey talk.

"When we're in the boat together, we only talk about fishing," Vince said. "It's all: 'remember that fish I caught that time?' That and country music."

And while Matt's career has taken him to another part of the continent, the Duchenes haven't been completely deprived of seeing their son in action. In fact, that first goal against

Detroit's Osgood came with the family in attendance at Joe Louis Arena. As an added bonus, they were sitting in a box with Mr. Hockey himself, Gordie Howe. Matt wears No. 9 for Colorado as a nod to the game's history. Both Howe and Maurice Richard made the digit famous and with his French-Canadian roots, Matt considers Richard a hero, even if he never saw him play live.

As part of a young Colorado team, Matt is quickly becoming an integral part of the Avs. He loves Denver and sees similarities to his home in Haliburton.

"I wouldn't say I'm a tree hugger, but I do love the outdoors," Matt said. "Denver's got the mountains and farmland...and it's got the country music, which I love."

It's fair to say that admiration goes both ways in the Rocky Mountain State. *– Ryan Kennedy*

★★★★★★★★★★★★★★★★★★★★★★★★★★★★★★★★★★

MATT DUCHENE'S FAVORITE [...] GROWING UP

JERSEY: CHICAGO BLACKHAWKS
MEMORABILIA: SIGNED PHOTO OF MAURICE RICHARD WITH THE STANLEY CUP
VIDEO GAME: EA SPORTS NHL SERIES
CARTOON: LOONIE TUNES
ALBUM: 21ST CENTURY BREAKDOWN BY GREEN DAY
MOVIE: WEDDING CRASHERS
SCHOOL SUBJECTS: ART AND GYM
JUNK FOOD: CHEESECAKE

★★★★★★★★★★★★★★★★★★★★★★★★★★★★★★★★★★

MILAN LUCIC

BOSTON BRUINS

POSITION: LEFT WING
DRAFTED: 50TH OVERALL IN 2006
BORN: JUNE 7, 1988 – VANCOUVER, B.C.
LAST DEVELOPMENTAL TEAM: VANCOUVER GIANTS (WHL)

Every single NHLer will tell you he's living the dream. But when Milan Lucic pinches himself he probably squeezes extra hard just to make sure things really won't go up in a puff of smoke.

In a relatively short period of time, Milan went from being passed over in the Western League bantam draft and wondering whether he had a future in the game at all to experiencing a series of hockey highs even some of the most accomplished players in the world would envy.

To top it off, each of his momentous achievements occurred right in his home city of Vancouver.

Milan grew up in B.C.'s largest center because his dad, Dobro, emigrated there from the former Yugoslavia in the mid-1980s, following the lead of his sister. Dobro was an accomplished soccer player in Europe, playing in what Milan described as the equivalent of the American Hockey League in Yugoslavia. In Vancouver, Dobro met and married another member of the city's Serbian community, a young woman named Snezana. Her brother, Dan Kesa, was an aspiring hockey player who ultimately played 139 games in the NHL.

With such strong sporting backgrounds on both sides of the family, it was no surprise that when Dobro and Snezana had kids, athletics quickly became part of the picture.

Milan is the middle child of three boys, one year younger than Jovan – who often played on the same youth hockey team with Milan – and two years older than Nikola.

From the first time he stepped on the ice, hockey was a way of life for Milan.

"In my head I was going to be an NHL hockey player," he said. "That was it."

The road to the pros wasn't always smooth however. In his early teens, the person who watched Milan closer than anyone on earth picked up on a problem that had the potential to shut the door on his hockey hopes.

"My mom more than anyone noticed that I didn't have correct posture," Milan said.

From the first time he stepped on the ice, hockey was a way of life for Milan.

Snezana's observation went beyond a mother thinking her son had to stop slouching. She followed up on her hunch and, around the time he was 14, Milan was diagnosed with spinal irregularity known as Scheuermann's disease. The condition causes a curvature of the spine in the upper back and while Milan says it sounds worse than it is, he still had to incorporate exercises into his routine to ensure things didn't deteriorate.

"You can't fully correct it because it is a curvature in your spine, but it's something that you can work at to maintain or get your posture back," he said. "If you let yourself go, your curvature gets worse and worse. That's when you start feeling more pain and create more problems for yourself.

"There were definitely days where it was tough dealing with it, but I didn't want to make it an excuse or a problem and it hasn't been up to this point."

In some ways, a stiffer test for Milan may have been maintaining belief in his abilities after his WHL draft snub.

"I was definitely crushed," he said. "That was the first time in my life where I did have some doubts about being a hockey player."

Exacerbating the problem was the fact Jr. B teams in the area were also unwilling to take a chance on Milan. But when coach Shane Kuss invited him into the Delta Ice Hawks fold, it was a perfect case of location, location, location. The Ice Hawks played their games in the Vancouver Giants' practice facility, meaning brass from the WHL club was often around.

MILAN LUCIC PLAYS IN BOSTON,
A TOWN THAT HAS FALLEN IN
LOVE WITH HIM FOR HIS CAM
NEELY-LIKE PLAY, BUT MOST OF
HIS FAVORITE MEMORIES HAVE
OCCURRED IN HIS HOMETOWN
OF VANCOUVER.

Always a banger and crasher, Milan's tough style stood out and earned him a spot on the Giants' list of protected players and he was given an opportunity to practice with the team during the 2004-05 campaign. Giants coach Don Hay, however, wasn't exactly blown away by his initial exposure to Milan and his skill set.

"Milan, as a young player, was what you'd call a project," Hay said. "He was a big, gangly guy, didn't really skate that well, didn't really do anything that well, other than work."

Milan's tenacity earned him an in-season bump from the Ice Hawks to Jr. A hockey with the Coquitlam Express of the British Columbia League. At the conclusion of that campaign, he dressed for a single Giants game and the next year became a full-time member.

"He came every day wanting to get better," Hay said, "almost challenging the coaches to make him better."

In his first WHL campaign, Milan collected 19 points in 62 games, while recording a robust 149 penalty minutes. Vancouver won the WHL title that year, but lost to the host Moncton Wildcats in the Memorial Cup semifinal.

Disappointing as that was, Milan's off-season was one to remember with the Boston Bruins selecting him in the second round, 50th overall, in the 2006 NHL draft – held, of course, in Vancouver. According to Milan, there's a direct correlation between the emptiness he felt after his first draft experience and the fact he put himself in a position to make the second one much more pleasurable.

"When all those teams pass up on you, you hear everyone say that you're not good enough and that's how it felt looking back on that day," he said of being passed over by WHL clubs. "But looking back now, the way that happened and getting passed up in the draft, it made me work that much harder in order to pursue my dream. It made me think that what I've been doing hasn't been good enough up to this point. Now what do I have to do to be good enough?"

After being drafted by the Bruins, Milan really amped up his game. With the Giants set to host the Memorial Cup in the spring of 2007, Milan notched 30 goals and 68 points in 70 games. He also proved to be a good leader and an all-around force on the team. Future Winnipeg Jet Evander Kane was a Giants rookie in Milan's last year with the team and said his older teammate was happy to take him under his wing.

"He was a guy who always talked to me, always gave me a bit of extra confidence, especially going into my first game," Kane said.

During the '07 post-season, Milan contributed 19 points in 22 contests, but couldn't prevent the Giants from being downed by the Medicine Hat Tigers in a seven-game WHL final.

> ## "It was special to win the Memorial Cup, but it was even more special to win it at home right beside the rink where I first started playing. It was an awesome, awesome, special event."
>
> # – Milan Lucic

However, Vancouver made good when it got another crack at the Tigers in the Memorial Cup final, posting a 3-1 victory to claim major junior hockey's most cherished trophy. To top it off, Milan was named tournament MVP.

"It was special to win it, but it was even more special to win it at home right beside the rink where I first started playing," Milan said. "It was an awesome, awesome, special event."

That summer, Milan was named captain of the Canadian team that dominated an eight-game exhibition series against junior-aged players from Russia that marked the 25th anniversary of the famous 1972 Summit Series. (The final contest of the series, a 6-0 Canada win in which Milan picked up an assist, was played in, where else, Vancouver.) He likely would have skated with many of those same Canadian kids at the 2008 World Junior Championship if not for the fact he managed to make the Boston Bruins as a 19-year-old that fall.

In four seasons with the Bruins, Milan has become a fan favorite with the blue-collar Boston faithful. At 6-foot-4 and 220 pounds, he's happy to hammer people into the end boards, but he also displays better-than-average goal-scoring ability – as evidenced by his 30 goals in 2010-11.

Milan's emergence as a multi-threat force that season was just part of what propelled Boston to its first Stanley Cup victory since 1972.

With goalie Tim Thomas leading the way, the Bruins capped a brilliant post-season by beating the Vancouver Canucks in the final, winning Game 7 in, you guessed it, Vancouver, to secure the title.

When he lifted the Cup over his head, Milan wasn't just completing an incredible hometown hat trick, he was putting the exclamation point on a journey that only a short time ago seemed as though it had gone off course.

"In seven years, I've been able to accomplish everything that every kid dreams of accomplishing," he said. "It's winning a Memorial Cup at home, it's being drafted in 2006 in Vancouver. And then I win a Stanley Cup here in Vancouver. I guess I could say that it's gone better than I ever dreamed of." – *Ryan Dixon*

★★★★★★★★★★★★★★★★★★★★★★★★★★★★★★★★★★

MILAN LUCIC'S FAVORITE [...] GROWING UP

PLAYER: PAVEL BURE
JERSEY: VANCOUVER CANUCKS (ALEXANDER MOGILNY)
CARTOON: THE SIMPSONS
ARTIST: METALLICA
MOVIE: DUMB AND DUMBER
VIDEO GAME: SUPER MARIO BROTHERS
SCHOOL SUBJECT: MATH

★★★★★★★★★★★★★★★★★★★★★★★★★★★★★★★★★★

ALEX PIETRANGELO

ST. LOUIS BLUES

POSITION: DEFENSE
DRAFTED: 4TH OVERALL IN 2008
BORN: JANUARY 18, 1990 – KING CITY, ONT.
LAST DEVELOPMENTAL TEAM: BARRIE COLTS (OHL)

A 16-year-old Alex Pietrangelo had just been taken third overall in the 2006 Ontario League draft and was about to make his debut with the Mississauga IceDogs. It was an exhibition game in Erie, Pa., about a four-hour drive from the Pietrangelo home in King City, Ont.

"I thought, 'You know what, I better go to this game,' " father Joe Pietrangelo remembered. "I said, 'I better go to this game because this may be the only game he ever plays. He may not play again.' "

Not only did Alex lace up his skates again, he became an OHL all-star, the top defenseman for Team Canada at the World Junior Championship and eventually one of the top young blueliners in the NHL for the St. Louis Blues. It's an adolescent athletic journey that found success because of Alex's ability to turn many perceived negatives into astonishing advantages.

"He wasn't good at accepting anything but the best he could do," Joe said. "That was just his thing. He worked at everything."

Alex didn't start skating until he was five years old. It took four weekends' worth of sessions before he stayed on the ice for one full skate. Still, he struggled. So when Alex finally started playing hockey, he hated it.

"Like any kid, if you're not good at something, you're not going to like doing it," Alex said. "My dad is not a hardcore hockey dad, but he said, 'You're good at it, just keep trying.' Once I got a little bit better, I fell in love with the sport."

Originally a forward, Alex switched to defense, but he was considered too defensive. His coach at the time, a terrific one according to the family, preached keeping the puck out of the net. But Alex had shown early signs of wanting to skate up ice, being more offense-minded, so Joe placed his son on the AAA Toronto Junior Canadiens, where he was coached by Tyler Craig.

"When I first saw Alex play, I was hesitant whether he would fit into the team play because he was so defensive," Craig said. "When I talked to his dad, I said, 'I like him, but he doesn't have any offense.' He said, 'That's exactly why I want him to come to you because I want him to learn, get in the play and become an offensive defenseman.'

"At 13, he was probably a point every fourth game. By that 14-15 range, that's when I really saw him start to take off. I thought, 'This guy has the ability to be a pro.' He was so smart at recognizing when to take those risks."

By then, Alex's name was gaining steam as one of the top picks in the 2006 OHL draft. His competition included guys named Steven Stamkos and Michael Del Zotto, whom Alex had grown up playing with and against. He preferred playing with them.

> ## "Alex wasn't good at accepting anything but the best he could do. That was just his thing. He worked at everything."
>
> # – Joe Pietrangelo

"It's a little intimidating as a kid when you see Stamkos coming down the ice," Alex said. "We lost one year to his team...it was like 9-1 and he had like seven or eight points. I was on the ice for almost every goal. A little demoralizing."

Sarnia had the No. 1 pick and took Stamkos. Oshawa followed at No. 2 and selected Del Zotto. That left Alex available at No. 3 and the pick belonged to Mississauga, a franchise struggling on the ice and facing a move to Niagara.

"Things fell where they fell," Joe said. "I told him, 'You go where you get drafted.' There were a lot of things that were negative, but we just accepted that that's the real world. You deal with it. If you've got the talent, they'll find you."

Alex quickly found the positive in his move to Mississauga. His mother, Edi, had cousins, Anna and Roy Rosset, who lived near the arena. Alex knew them well enough that he referred to them as his aunt and uncle. The familiarity eased his transition.

"When you're 16 and you go into a family you don't know and you're still in high school, it's hard," Alex said. "But to have them there, they were so supportive...I was lucky."

His parents were more comfortable, too.

"(The Rossets) had pre-teens, so they understood all the stuff that could go on," Joe said. "You think about these kids leaving the house at 15-16 years old, they're pretty young. If they get into a bunch of rotten apples, you hope they're a little wiser than that. But until they experience that, it's pretty tough to tell."

Alex admitted he wasn't perfect.

"I got caught out one time," he said, "my aunt was saying, 'It's a little late for you.' You're 16 years old and you're hanging out with teammates who are 20-year-olds. Sometimes you get ahead of yourself."

Alex was getting ahead of himself on the ice, too. He was six-feet tall and had skills to match, netting 52 points in 59 games as a rookie.

"I thought, 'There's a possibility that I can make this a living,' " Alex said. "Everybody in junior hockey thinks they have a chance to make the NHL and they all do. You have to believe in yourself; that's all it comes down to."

Joe saw that in Alex's first OHL game at Erie.

"Boy, was I surprised," he said. "He just wasn't afraid to play. I could just see that he didn't hold back. He played his game and you can see that he had the confidence to play at that level."

When Alex's performance did dip, he heard from his former coach.

> ## "Everybody in junior hockey thinks they have a chance to make the NHL and they all do. You have to believe in yourself; that's all it comes down to."
>
> ## – Alex Pietrangelo

HE'S BIG. HE'S POWERFUL.
HE CAN PLAY IN BOTH ENDS.
WHAT'S NOT TO LIKE ABOUT
ALEX PIETRANGELO? BLUES FANS
WILL TELL YOU THEY LOVE
EVERYTHING ABOUT
THEIR NO. 1 BLUELINER.

"It gets awful lonely when things aren't going well," Craig said. "But you just say, 'Hey, you're doing that thing where you're trying to be too defensive because you're trying not to make a mistake. That's not you; you've got to be more aggressive.' Just little words of wisdom."

Alex then lost some of his comfort zone. The Mississauga franchise did move to Niagara, meaning Alex had to move from his relatives' home. But by that time, he had built a foundation.

"Mississauga was good, but my two big years were in Niagara," he said. "It's an awesome city. We had great support. Things didn't really pan out in terms of winning, but it was the first team I got really close to."

Hockey players love their pranks and the IceDogs were no exception.

"We used to put our trainer's car on cinder blocks after practice," Alex said. "It was a little over the top, but we got a chuckle out of it."

In 2008, however, hockey became serious. The kid who didn't enjoy the game initially wound up as the No. 4 overall pick in the NHL draft. Expectations were high. But despite two cracks at the St. Louis roster as an 18- and 19-year-old prospect, the team sent Alex to the World Junior Championship and then back to his junior team.

Once again, Alex turned the circumstances in his favor. In 2010, he was named the top defenseman at the WJC.

"Are you disappointed?" Joe asked. "Yes, of course. But I always thought, 'You want to get there and you want to stay there.' It was the best thing for him."

Added Alex: "For any kid who gets to be a part of that tournament, it's an awesome experience. You always want to play in the NHL, but now that you look back, it's only going to help you."

In 2011, Alex suited up for Team Canada again, this time for the IIHF World Championship in Slovakia. Back home, he had someone watching his every move.

"I clipped some video of Alex and showed it to the kids I'm coaching now," Craig said. "He was the 'off' defenseman and was covering the front of the net. His partner was battling the puck in the corner and there was a turnover. Alex jumped up in the rush, got the puck and had a great scoring opportunity. I'd love to say I coached that, but that's something he recognized on his own."

Craig wouldn't take credit. Just like the Pietrangelos would never take credit for where Alex is now.

"We're a pretty humble group," Joe said. "We weren't looking at the big picture before he could skate. They all have dreams. Was there a specific moment where Alex said he was going to be in the NHL? No. But he did talk about it and we always told him, 'Work hard at whatever you do.' "

It's still the same today." – *Jeremy Rutherford*

★★★★★★★★★★★★★★★★★★★★★★★★★★★★★★★★★★

ALEX PIETRANGELO'S FAVORITE [...] GROWING UP

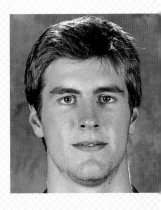

PLAYER: NICKLAS LIDSTROM
CARTOON: FAMILY GUY
ARTIST: BRAD PAISLEY
MOVIE: HANGOVER
VIDEO GAME: CALL OF DUTY
SPORT OTHER THAN HOCKEY: GOLF
SCHOOL SUBJECT: MATH
JUNK FOOD: OREOS

★★★★★★★★★★★★★★★★★★★★★★★★★★★★★★★★★★

89

JAMES VAN RIEMSDYK

PHILADELPHIA FLYERS

POSITION: LEFT WING

DRAFTED: 2ND OVERALL IN 2007

BORN: MAY 4, 1989 – MIDDLETOWN, N.J.

LAST DEVELOPMENTAL TEAM: NEW HAMPSHIRE WILDCATS (HE)

As you'd expect with a future NHLer, James van Riemsdyk was always a bit ahead of the pack when he was a kid. He was big from the beginning and those soft hands always had a way of separating him from the crowd. But there was one area of the arena where James dragged hopelessly behind: the dressing room.

Alex DePalma coached James through the majority of his youth hockey days, often alongside James' dad. DePalma recalls the days when James' young teammates would be ready to charge onto the ice, giving each other the final fist pounds and shin-pad taps before battle, while the club's most talented player was lagging behind, putting on his equipment with the care of a 16-year-old girl going to the spring formal.

"Everybody would have their pants and skates on and James was still pulling up his socks," DePalma said. "He was so meticulous that I'd have to tell his father, 'Go wait outside the locker room,' and I'd say, 'James, will you pull up your socks already!' Everything had to be just right."

James may now be a 6-foot-3, 200-pound power forward for the Philadelphia Flyers, but in some ways, nothing has changed from those days playing for the Shore Selects in Brick, N.J.

"I always had to have my stuff fitting the right way, I'm still the same way now," James laughed. "I'm probably one of the slowest dressers of all-time."

DePalma says James' attention to detail extended beyond his own equipment. He claims, as a youngster, James knew what everyone on his team was wearing and holding, an indication of just how focused he was on all aspects of the game right from the beginning. His determined nature made him tough to stop on the ice, but also provided his teammates with a fun challenge off of it.

"The thing was to get James to laugh and get that smile because he was very serious," DePalma said.

He was also very loyal. The Shore Selects were the equivalent of an AA team, but as his talents became more and more obvious, James was asked constantly to join AAA teams in the area. He always opted to stay, partly because he built such a strong bond playing year after year with the same kids, some of whom are still in his close circle and can be found watching their old buddy play with the big boys just down the road a bit in Philadelphia. James is convinced his development was aided by the fact hockey with his friends was always fun.

> # "I always had to have my stuff fitting the right way, I'm still the same way now. I'm probably one of the slowest dressers of all-time."
>
> # – James van Riemsdyk

"That's kind of a special thing I think," James said. "Especially today when you have some crazy parents treating youth hockey like it's the NHL, trying to switch organizations every year and all this other stuff."

While James found a great circle of friends through hockey, the game didn't necessarily occupy a prominent spot on the New Jersey sporting landscape.

"Typically here in the States and in New Jersey, when kids are able to take their first couple steps, the next thing that follows is a simple game of catch and then out comes the Wiffle Ball bat," said James' father, Frans.

But family history had a little bit to do with James adopting hockey as his passion. Frans' parents moved to North America from Holland in the late 1950s and the fact he was born in Montreal carried some inherent responsibilities with it.

"My father sort of said, 'You're the designated Canadian in the family and part of your heritage has to be, you have to embrace the game of hockey,' " Frans explained.

Warming to the game was no trouble, as Frans quickly became an avid hockey-watcher and occasional player. With a father who worked for the international banking arm of American Express, moves became quite common for Frans over the years, but he eventually settled as an adult in New Jersey.

When James, the oldest of three boys, was born, some remnants of Frans' hockey background were within a toddler's reach.

"It just so happened we had a couple of these plastic mini-sticks and we couldn't get it out of his hands," Frans said. "It wasn't all a fun story because he'd wildly swing this thing around, often to the great irritation of grandparents and friends who were around getting whacked in the shin by this little kid."

James remembers his mini-stick well; it was adorned with the name and logo of his favorite team growing up, the New York Rangers. The other item that pulled him into the game before he could even really form words was an old VHS tape called *Wayne Gretzky: Above and Beyond*.

"I don't think he was able to speak clearly yet, he was that young, but he would mutter the title of the video and for weeks we couldn't figure out what the heck he was talking about," Frans said. "And then we said, 'My God, I think he's talking about the title of this Gretzky video.' "

That wasn't the only time James communicated his zeal for the game to his dad. Once he began playing organized hockey, James was on the ice all the time, not just in the winter, but also while competing for summer select teams. One year, fearing James might lose his lust for the sport if he became over-exposed, Frans suggested his son skip a tryout for a summer club in favor of spending a nice Mother's Day with the family. The plan was not well received.

"He was beside himself," Frans said. "That was the first sign of him being really passionate about it."

After his youth hockey days with the Shore Selects, James made the move to high school hockey and scored 36 goals and 60 points in 30 games for Christian Brothers Academy in 2004-05. He spent the next two seasons with the U.S. national team development program based in Ann Arbor, Mich., where his reputation really began to grow.

PART OF A NEW BREED
OF POWER FORWARDS
WHO COMBINE SIZE
WITH SPEED, JAMES
VAN RIEMSDYK
– 'JVR' AS HE'S QUICKLY
BECOME KNOWN –
IS A HANDFUL FOR
DEFENDERS.

James spent the 2006-07 campaign with the U.S. NTDP under-18 squad and became a dominant offensive force, averaging 1.6 points-per-game for the team in 58 contests versus a wide variety of international, NCAA and North American League competition. That caught the eye of the Flyers organization, which finished last in the league during that NHL season, but held the No. 2 overall pick in the draft after the Chicago Blackhawks won the lottery.

As is the case with most players, James was nervous on the eve of the big event, but he became much more settled after a conversation with Philadelphia's management.

> **"The one thing I remember about the draft is visiting with the Flyers before and they told me if I was still on the board at No. 2 they were going to take me there"**
>
> **— James van Riemsdyk**

"The one thing I remember is visiting with the Flyers before and they told me if I was still on the board at No. 2 they were going to take me there," he said. "Obviously you never really know, but that helped ease my mind a bit going into it and relax and enjoy the whole experience a little more."

True to its word, Philly took James right after the Hawks snatched Patrick Kane with the No. 1 pick, marking the first time Americans had gone 1-2 in the draft.

Unlike Kane, who moved straight to the NHL the next season, James spent two years honing his skills at the University of New Hampshire. Despite that apprenticeship, James had some trouble adjusting his game to the NHL level when it was time to go pro. He tallied a decent 15 goals during an up-and-down rookie season in 2009-10, which included a trip to the Cup final, where the Flyers were downed by Kane and the Hawks. But as a second-year player, James found his footing, taking advantage of increased opportunity and, in turn, a confidence boost to start realizing his potential as a big man on the left wing with ample scoring touch. His goal total jumped to 21 tallies. Then he scored seven more in 11 playoff games.

To the detriment of his odometer and morning schedule, Frans frequently makes the hour-and-a-half trek to see his son skate for the Flyers. He also has plenty of other action to keep an eye on because James' brothers are following the path he blazed. Trevor van Riemsdyk also attended Christian Brothers Academy and was set to begin his freshman year at his brother's NCAA alma mater, New Hampshire, in the fall of 2011. Brendan, the youngest, is still in the midst of his Christian Brothers career.

As for James, the entire hockey world is starting to realize what his old coach was able to spot right away when a rangy, resolute kid graduated from mini-sticks to the real deal.

"Somebody said to me a long time ago, 'Goal-scorers see net, the rest of us see the goalie,'" DePalma said. "James saw net." – *Ryan Dixon*

★★★★★★★★★★★★★★★★★★★★★★★★★★★★★★★★★★★★

JAMES VAN RIEMSDYK'S FAVORITE [...] GROWING UP

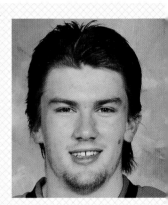

PLAYER: ADAM GRAVES
JERSEYS: NEW YORK RANGERS AND ATLANTA THRASHERS
CARTOON: HEY ARNOLD!
ARTIST: JOHN MAYER
MOVIE: THE HANGOVER
VIDEO GAME: EA SPORTS NHL SERIES
SPORT OTHER THAN HOCKEY: TENNIS
SCHOOL SUBJECT: MATH
JUNK FOOD: PIZZA

★★★★★★★★★★★★★★★★★★★★★★★★★★★★★★★★★★★★

VICTOR HEDMAN

TAMPA BAY LIGHTNING

POSITION: DEFENSE

DRAFTED: 2ND OVERALL IN 2009

BORN: DECEMBER 18, 1990 – ORNSKOLDSVIK, SWEDEN

LAST DEVELOPMENTAL TEAM: MODO (SWEDEN)

The hype that surrounded Victor Hedman leading up to the 2009 draft was only surpassed by the player eventually taken ahead of him – John Tavares, the phenom hockey fans had been anticipating for years in advance. But there was also a lot of buzz around the 6-foot-6 Swedish blueliner who could really move out on the ice.

It was all a lot to take in for a kid who grew up in a small yet hockey-mad town on the Swedish coast. Hailing from Ornskoldsvik, Victor was joining a parade of elite local players such as Peter Forsberg, Henrik and Daniel Sedin and Markus Naslund. Despite all that talent, Ornskoldsvik is far from a metropolis. Victor lived on his own for two years while playing for the town's fabled Modo squad and it wasn't hard to get around.

"From my apartment," Victor said, "it was a two-minute walk downtown and two minutes to the rink."

But that hominess also helped foster a love of sport as the big Swede grew up.

Victor describes the town of 35,000 as a great place to play soccer in the summer and a wonderland in winter, where ice is everywhere and the skiing is solid. When he wasn't outside playing hockey, Victor was often in the basement trading slashes with his two older brothers, Oscar and Johan. As with any sibling rivalry, Victor took the brunt of it most days as the youngest.

"Tell me about it," he said. "It would always end with me crying and running upstairs, but the next day I was back down there."

Olle Hedman, the father of the clan and a former goalie himself, believes that young pluck has stuck with Victor to this day.

"He's very consistent," Olle said. "When he wants to do something, he does it. He liked to compete with his brothers. There was a lot of crying...they were hard on him."

But as the years went on, Victor's size made him tougher to pick on. Olle remembers Victor always being big, but really taking off at 11 years old. The blueliner estimates that he broke the six-foot barrier around age 13 and getting used to his body was a process.

"I was growing faster and faster," Victor recalled. "It took time for me to develop good co-ordination, as well as my skating and muscle."

> ## "There was a lot of crying… Victor's brothers were hard on him."
> # – Olle Hedman

He now dwarfs Oscar, a 6-foot, 207-pound blueliner and Washington Capitals draftee who played a year with Victor in Modo before getting traded to Frolunda before the 2008-09 season.

"My brother is very important to me," Victor said. "We talk almost every day. It's a great friendship."

Another important person in Victor's life then was Modo defense partner and mentor Mattias Timander, a veteran of more than 400 NHL games, mostly with Boston and Columbus.

"He's a great player still," Victor said. "He gave me a lot of tips for every situation on the ice and off the ice."

Timander, as a defensive stalwart, also gave Victor the opportunity to roam up ice when the chance came, allowing the youngster to flourish as a two-way defenseman who loves to rush the puck.

"He lets you do your thing," Victor said.

The first time North Americans got a really good look at the wunderkind blueliner was at the 2009 World Junior Championship in Ottawa. Though his two assists in six games isn't exactly a world-beating total, there may be a good explanation.

VICTOR HEDMAN, WHOSE STEADY, POWERFUL PLAY IN SWEDEN MADE HIM THE SECOND-OVERALL DRAFT PICK IN 2009, WILL PLAY A BIG ROLE IN GETTING THE LIGHTNING BACK TO THE STANLEY CUP.

According to Olle, who also happened to be in his second decade as equipment manager of Sweden's under-20s, the Swedish game plan limited Victor. With David Rundblad, Erik Karlsson and Tim Erixon playing as the offensive defenseman, Victor was expected to hang back more than he would with Modo.

"He wasn't allowed to play his normal game," Olle theorized. "But he did what they wanted him to do."

For Victor, the silver medal and the experience playing on an NHL-sized rink still paid off.

"I really liked the smaller ice," he said. "You need to know what you're going to do with the puck."

And though the Swedes fell short of their goal of a gold medal, Victor also got an in-your-face tutorial to North American hockey courtesy the champion Canadians.

"Canada always plays full-speed – I really like how they played," Victor said. "We didn't come up to our standard, but Canada was very good."

If there was one area Victor got a chance to prove himself in during that contentious final, it was the questions surrounding his snarl – or lack thereof.

But in a game where goalie and close friend Jacob Markstrom had more than a few up-close-and-personal moments with Canadian forecheckers, Victor did not just stand idly by. Specifically, he put Atlanta Thrashers prospect Angelo Esposito in a headlock after the pivot collided with Markstrom by the right faceoff dot.

"If you touch my goalie, I'm going to go after you," Victor said matter-of-factly. "I could have done a lot more to him, but I wanted to stay in the game. I did do enough for 20,000 people to boo me every time I touched the puck, though."

But there was no booing when the Tampa Bay Lightning selected Victor second overall at the draft that summer. Getting picked right after Tavares meant history was written the way it had been predicted, but Victor was still pleased.

"Deep inside, I really wanted to go to Tampa, because I knew they were interested in me," he said.

Victor and his girlfriend made the move to Florida from Sweden, which meant more than just getting used to the opposite weather patterns; it was a whole culture change. On top of that, the Lightning organization was in shambles at the time, with inexperienced owners Oren Koules and Len Barrie struggling at the helm.

> "Deep inside, I really wanted to go to Tampa, because I knew they were interested in me."
>
> **– Victor Hedman**

Given it all, Victor's rookie totals of 20 points and a minus-3 rating in 74 games weren't so bad and the youngster was happy to have that sort of trial to go through.

"It was an important year," Victor said. "The first year is always tough and everything is new. I felt I needed to improve over the summer...you always want to be a complete player, but it takes time."

And just as he could lean on Timander back home, Victor benefited from being around fellow Swedish defenseman Mattias Ohlund in Tampa.

"He really helped me on the ice and off the ice," Victor said. "He took care of me right away."

For his sophomore season in Tampa, Victor saw a good chunk of the organization swept away as Jeff Vinik bought the team from Koules and Barrie, installing NHL legend Steve Yzerman as GM. Yzerman then brought on Guy Boucher as the team's rookie coach and the Bolts turned a corner.

Victor showed improvement under the new regime, besting his rookie year totals in assists, points and plus-minus, while logging 21 minutes of ice time per night. With the Lightning returning to the playoffs for the first time since 2007,

Victor once again stepped up his game and learned a lot in the process.

"Everything was so much fun," he said. "They're the games you watch when you're young."

Tampa got to the Eastern Conference final before losing to the eventual champs from Boston and the roller coaster is still fresh in Victor's mind.

"Coming back to beat Pittsburgh in the first round after being down three games to one and obviously beating the Capitals in four – those are big memories," he said. "I still haven't forgotten the loss to Boston in Game 7. The taste of the seventh game isn't going away."

Fortunately, Victor still has a long and positive-looking future ahead of him in the NHL. Funny thing is, if he hadn't become an elite hockey player, the youngster from Ornskoldsvik had other designs for a career.

"I wanted to be a pilot," he said.

And though it's tough to picture Victor crammed into a cockpit, there's always the days after retirement for the big Swede to fulfill that dream. In the meantime, the Lightning defenseman will surely settle for soaring in the NHL and the means to chase that oh-so-coveted Stanley Cup. Thankfully, his coach already saw a lot of growth in Victor during their first season together.

"I saw a kid that became a man," Boucher said. "Those guys that are drafted so high, they always feel they need to put up offensive numbers to back up their ranking and I think he understood this year that's not what he has to do."

It was a lesson in maturity for Victor, one he clearly passed.

"By Christmas time he realized that whenever he played a stable game he looked so good out there," Boucher said. "He's not forcing the play. Defensemen are outstanding not because they do outstanding things, but because they have consistency and efficiency. That's what the top guys do."
– *Ryan Kennedy*

★★★★★★★★★★★★★★★★★★★★★★★★★★★★★★★★★

VICTOR HEDMAN'S FAVORITE [...] GROWING UP

PLAYER: PETER FORSBERG
JERSEY: MODO
MEMORABILIA: STICKS FROM FORSBERG, THE SEDIN BROS. AND MARKUS NASLUND
CARTOON: SCOOBY-DOO
MOVIE: THE HANGOVER
VIDEO GAMES: EA SPORTS FIFA SOCCER SERIES, CALL OF DUTY
SPORT OTHER THAN HOCKEY: SOCCER
SCHOOL SUBJECT: ENGLISH
JUNK FOOD: SWEDISH PIZZA (THINNER THAN AMERICAN)

★★★★★★★★★★★★★★★★★★★★★★★★★★★★★★★★★

PATRICK KANE

CHICAGO BLACKHAWKS

POSITION: RIGHT WING
DRAFTED: 1ST OVERALL IN 2007
BORN: NOVEMBER 19, 1988 – BUFFALO, N.Y.
LAST DEVELOPMENTAL TEAM: LONDON KNIGHTS (OHL)

When Patrick Kane takes to the ice in Buffalo, there are always mixed emotions. Sure, he's one of the better players ever to come out of the city, but playing for the Chicago Blackhawks, he's wearing the enemy sweater at HSBC Arena.

Turns out, that's not a recent phenomenon. Patrick's family had season tickets to the Sabres when he was growing up and even though he cheered for Buffalo, the future Calder Trophy winner had it in his head that it was fun to wear the opposing team's sweater to games.

"I think he had just about every team," said Donna Kane, Patrick's mom. "And it was like, 'Seriously, Patrick, you have to wear *that* one tonight?' "

Thanks to his young age, Patrick was never prodded too much about wearing enemy colors and in fact, he often made new friends at the Sabres' old arena, the raucous Buffalo Memorial Auditorium. Patrick would bring his mini-stick to games and every intermission he'd get a game going with other kids in attendance.

"He used to play mini-sticks all the time in the living room," Donna said. "He and his father would have knock-down, drag'em-out games, but Patrick would also get his sisters to play or me or his uncle."

Once Patrick started playing hockey at age seven, he didn't stop – almost literally. He would sometimes change sweaters in the car while his dad, Pat Sr., drove him to another rink.

"I played on so many teams I didn't know what game I was going to sometimes," Patrick said. "I was on seven teams one year, counting summer hockey."

When Patrick wasn't on the ice or playing mini-sticks or at a Sabres game – or at a Sabres game playing mini-sticks – he was playing road hockey. The Kanes lived on a quiet street, making it a perfect place to set up a net without the need to yell "Car!" every two minutes. And though Patrick was a very happy kid, he was also quite serious and competitive about his hockey, even on the street.

Donna recalls more than one instance of seeing her son roll by the front window with his roller blades on, net in hand, just minutes after heading out to play with other kids on the block.

"He'd come in and say, 'They're just goofing around out there, I'm trying to play a real game,' " Donna said. "I would say 'Patrick. It's street hockey.' He'd sulk for a bit, but then he'd be right back out there."

On the ice, Patrick was a whiz. In addition to his speed and skills as a hockey player, he also had an extra layer of intimidation – he liked to paint every piece of his gear black, including the name on his skates and stick.

"You could tell how bad he got hit in a game by how much we had to re-paint after," Donna said.

Patrick's skill set did not go unnoticed. After an MVP performance at a tournament in Toronto, the eighth grader was getting courted heavily by the Detroit Honeybaked program, one of the top outfits in Michigan and a noted developer of NHL talent. Former NHLer Pat Verbeek was the assistant coach of the team, which included his son, Kyle. Recognizing the whole Kane clan was unsure of sending their son out of state at such a young age, Verbeek offered to billet Patrick himself. That Kyle and Patrick got along so well helped. Both were the oldest kids in their family and Kyle has four sisters – Patrick has three.

"It was a sacrifice that had to be made," Patrick said.

> "I played on so many teams I didn't know what game I was going to sometimes. I was on seven teams one year, counting summer hockey."
>
> **– Patrick Kane**

AS A KID GROWING UP IN BUFFALO, PATRICK KANE WAS VERY SERIOUS ABOUT HOCKEY – EVEN IF HE WAS JUST PLAYING ON THE STREET WITH FRIENDS.

But not one without heartache. Patrick had stayed with the Verbeeks for a weekend as a test run, but when the final goodbyes had to be said, it was a different story. Donna had just returned home with her sister from dropping her son off when she got a phone call: Patrick wanted to come back.

"I wanted to turn that car around to go get him," Donna said. "But I told him, 'Pat, we're not quitters in this family. You've got to at least try it.'"

To his credit, Patrick did just that and as it turns out, the decision worked out for the best. He was playing for a top-tier team and getting to live with a good friend whose dad just happened to have lived the NHL dream Patrick was chasing.

"It was awesome," Patrick said. "Me and Kyle used to wrestle him. He'll say he never lost, but I think we got him down at least once or twice."

The Honeybaked program was a great stepping-stone in Patrick's career, though there was one rather ironic low in the experience. After claiming the state title in Michigan, the club went on to the nationals. Undefeated in the round robin, Honeybaked met up with the Buffalo Regals in the semifinal – the team Patrick would have played for had he stayed at home. Honeybaked had beaten the Regals soundly in the round robin, but Buffalo got the last laugh when it mattered, ending the Detroit squad's tournament.

There weren't many disappointments for Patrick after that. Though he flirted with the idea of playing college hockey – his buddy Brett Bennett was going to Boston University and Michigan was also a possibility – Patrick decided to play major junior, forming a devastating line with fellow future NHLers Sam Gagner and Sergei Kostitsyn on the Ontario League's London Knights.

Over the course of the 2006-07 season the trio combined for nearly 400 points, with Patrick leading the league with 145 in just 58 games. Run by former NHLers Dale and Mark Hunter, Patrick and friends found a perfect situation for their high-octane skills.

"The Hunters were a lot of fun to play for," Patrick said. "They would just let us run and gun. They'd have you on the power play for the full two minutes."

And the admiration ran both ways. Mark Hunter, the GM of the Knights, recalled sitting down with Patrick after his first 10 games – a span in which the young American had nine goals.

"We knew he was a special kid and a driven kid," Hunter said. "We sat him down to see how he felt about his play and he said, 'I can be better.' He just took off from there. When you saw that kind of push, you knew he was special."

So special in fact, he was selected first overall in the 2007 draft. Always big on family, Patrick had a huge cheering section in Columbus – about 100 folks in total – and they came prepared. When Donna had told her sister at the beginning of the season that Patrick was slated to go in the first three rounds, word went viral amongst the extended family.

"They all had their hotel rooms by January," Donna laughed.

A cottage industry of conspiracy theories has sprung up in trying to find an explanation, but the Patrick Kane's Stanley Cup-winning puck has yet to be found.

But after a sizzling World Junior Championship for Team USA and continued excellence in London, Patrick's stock was soaring. He and his mom flew out to the CHL awards in Vancouver, where he had won rookie-of-the-year honors. There, they had a chance encounter with Chicago Blackhawks GM Dale Tallon. It was still May, but Tallon told them point-blank he planned on taking Patrick with the first pick overall.

Of course, the Kanes had to wait another month to confirm that claim, but Tallon was true to his word and with previous first-rounder Jonathan Toews ready for NHL action, the Hawks had a dynamic duo en route to a pretty speedy rebuild. Patrick and Toews quickly gelled on and off the ice.

"We have a lot of fun together," Patrick said. "Once a game we'll get mad at each other, but a couple shifts later we'll score. We'll still be mad at each other, but it's all good."

And it was definitely all good when the pair won the Stanley Cup for Chicago in 2010. Ending 49 years of misery for Hawks fans will do that, even if the winning goal that Patrick scored was an odd one.

Patrick's overtime winner in Game 6 against Philadelphia was unique in that very few people actually saw it sneak past goalie Michael Leighton at first.

"We were sitting on (Chicago goalie) Antti Niemi's side of the building," Donna said. "Next thing we know, Patrick has thrown his gloves in the air and my husband said 'Oh great, Patrick's making a fool of himself in front of millions of people.' We never saw the goal – they didn't replay it on the Jumbotron."

But Patrick knew it was in. The only problem was what happened to the puck after. A cottage industry of conspiracy theories has sprung up in trying to find an explanation, but the puck has yet to be found.

"I guess they're still trying to figure that out," Patrick said. "I'd like to see it come back to Chicago because of the history and it being 49 years since the last Cup."

But Patrick will always have one thing to treasure – the ability to chirp his buddy Toews about the way the final ended.

"The joke between us is that I was the last guy off the bench because I wanted to be 100 percent sure it was in," Toews said. "He'll say it's because I wanted to score the goal."

Maybe next time. – *Ryan Kennedy*

★★★★★★★★★★★★★★★★★★★★★★★★★★★★★★★★★★

PATRICK KANE'S FAVORITE […] GROWING UP

JERSEY: BUFFALO SABRES
MEMORABILIA: BIG BINDER OF HOCKEY CARDS
VIDEO GAME: EA SPORTS NHL SERIES
CARTOON: BOBBY'S WORLD
MOVIE: BATMAN RETURNS
SCHOOL SUBJECT: GYM
JUNK FOOD: TWIZZLERS

★★★★★★★★★★★★★★★★★★★★★★★★★★★★★★★★★★

CLAUDE GIROUX

PHILADELPHIA FLYERS

POSITION: CENTER

DRAFTED: 22ND OVERALL IN 2006

BORN: JANUARY 12, 1988 – HEARST, ONT.

LAST DEVELOPMENTAL TEAM: GATINEAU OLYMPIQUES (QMJHL)

Ray Giroux knows some very good hockey players have come out of Hearst. The problem is they also tend to come back.

Hearst is a Northern Ontario town of about 6,000 people situated along Highway 11. If you're driving anywhere from there, your destination can't be much farther north because, latitude-wise, Hearst is one of the last places accessible by road in the area. Drive nearly eight hours south and you'll hit Sault Ste. Marie while about the same amount of time in the car will get you to Thunder Bay if you're headed west.

But when it comes to talented players packing up and leaving Hearst to see how they stack up in bigger centers, all roads seem to lead back home.

"It's not because they weren't good," Ray said. "It's because they miss their small town."

Claude Giroux's early days in hockey were probably very similar to those of the guys his father Ray was referencing. He learned to love the game the way many young kids do, simply by playing on icy streets and frozen ponds around the neighborhood. Even before he was two years old, Claude was glued to the action when hockey was on TV. When intermissions intruded on the fun, he simply turned his focus elsewhere.

"He didn't relax," Ray said. "The stick came out and I had to play with him."

That was a common theme in the Giroux household because Claude's older sister, Isabelle, was also an avid hockey player. Five years Claude's senior, Isabelle was an accomplished enough player that at 15, she took that long journey from home to spend a season playing for the Thunder Bay Queens. That program has turned out a number of players who've suited up in university or college hockey in Canada and the U.S., including Haley Irwin, who won gold with Canada at the 2010 Olympics.

Like many older sisters, Isabelle was often asked to babysit her little brother, which she invariably knew would lead to another question, this time from Claude about whether or not she wanted to play hockey.

"It's basically what he wanted to do," Isabelle said.

Always happy to oblige, Isabelle, a blueliner by trade, was probably one of the first defenders in the game to find out how hard it can be to try and stop Claude from creating offense.

"He actually was pretty happy to be against me, because he knew what to do and what my weaknesses were," she said with a laugh.

As time passed and Claude's skills became apparent to anyone paying attention, Ray began thinking about the circular path some of Hearst's other talented players had taken. He couldn't help but wonder if it would be the same story for Claude.

"We knew it was just a question of time when he was going to move out and come back, just like the other guys," Ray said.

So he came up with a solution; the whole family would move. With Isabelle already doing her post-secondary studies in Ottawa, the entire Giroux clan made the nearly 1,000-kilometer move southeast to the city. Ray, an electrician, knew his skills would still be in demand, while Claude, 14 at the time, could hone his hockey chops against better competition.

> "He was so small, he was a late-bloomer, so it was not even on our mind that he would make the NHL."
>
> **— Ray Giroux**

Claude acknowledged it was tough leaving all his close friends behind, but he quickly found a new group of buddies on the ice. While his playmaking talents certainly stood out, Claude was anything but a blue-chipper. At 5-foot-11 and 172 pounds now, Giroux is undersized by NHL standards and was definitely one of the smaller kids growing up.

"At that time I never thought Claude would make the NHL," Ray said. "He was so small, he was a late-bloomer, so it was not even on our mind that he would make the NHL."

Forget the big show, even playing major junior hockey looked improbable after Claude was passed over in his Ontario League draft year. But it was while playing Jr. A hockey for the Cumberland Grads in 2004-05 that Claude caught the attention of Rick Julien, the older brother of Boston Bruins coach and Stanley Cup-winner Claude Julien. Rick wasn't directly involved in hockey, but obviously it was in his family genes. He knew an owner with the Quebec League's Gatineau Olympiques – right across the river from Ottawa – and suggested somebody come watch this Giroux kid play. So, Olympiques coach Benoit Groulx did just that.

While the coach was by no means blown away by what he saw, Claude demonstrated enough potential to earn an invite to Gatineau's training camp the following autumn. Shortly thereafter, Groulx knew he had a player on his hands.

"It took us about 48 hours to know he was the best rookie at our camp that year," he said.

Groulx may have immediately spotted Claude's potential, but that doesn't mean the process of extracting it was always smooth. With the benefit of hindsight, Claude is very blunt when accessing the state of his game and attitude at the outset of his major junior career.

"I was kind of a lazy guy when I went there, I was kind of soft," he said. "(Groulx) really focused on my work ethic and he wouldn't let me be lazy. Not that I didn't like him, but he was all over me, so it was kind of tough. But that's why he's a good coach, because he knows how to push his players."

Claude heaps a ton of credit on Groulx and the Gatineau program for getting him directed and setting him on the path to NHL stardom, so much so that he wonders how things may have played out had he actually been drafted by an OHL club when he was eligible, instead of taking the long way around and joining the Olympiques.

"If I had have been drafted, maybe I wouldn't be where I am right now," he said.

With some prodding from Groulx and playing on a team that also featured future Bruins star David Krejci, Claude had an outstanding rookie season, notching 103 points in 69 games

AFTER THE FLYERS DEALT CAPTAIN MIKE RICHARDS AND SNIPER JEFF CARTER IN THE SUMMER OF 2011, CLAUDE GIROUX WAS LOOKED UPON TO BECOME A TOP DOG FOR PHILLY.

to make the QMJHL all-rookie team. That performance, naturally, caught the attention of a few NHL teams as they prepared for the 2006 draft.

Prior to the big day, two of the clubs Claude met with were the New York Rangers and the team he grew up rooting for, the Montreal Canadiens. The Habs held the 20th overall pick in the draft, while the Rangers were next at No. 21. Based on his interaction with the two teams, Claude thought he was destined to be wearing a uniform that prominently featured red and blue. But once again, being passed over turned out to be a blessing in disguise.

> ## Claude Giroux thought he was destined to be wearing a uniform that prominently featured red and blue. But once again, being passed over turned out to be a blessing in disguise.

"I really thought I was going to go to one or the other and when they both passed me I didn't know where I was going to go," he said. "Philly was up next and I'm pretty happy to be where I'm at right now."

Before becoming a full-time Flyer, Claude still had some things to prove in junior. Groulx believes Claude rested on his laurels a bit after being drafted and while he was still a prodigious point-getter as a 'Q' sophomore, Groulx knew Claude had more to give.

"We had a meeting at the end of that second year and told him we weren't really pleased with not only his work ethic, but the way he worked at getting better as a hockey player and the way he took care of his career," Groulx said. "He understood and we saw a big change in his last year."

The result was a magical season in which Claude won gold with Canada at the World Junior Championship, then went absolutely crazy in the Quebec League playoffs, scoring 51 points in 19 games to lead Gatineau to a league title. While the Olympiques failed to win a game at the Memorial Cup, Claude showed the world what kind of game he had.

"From Day 1 to the Memorial Cup, he was our best player," Groulx said. "And he was not only our best player, he was a leader."

Giroux's coming-out party in the NHL occurred when he notched 21 points in 23 games as a sophomore during the Flyers' run to the 2010 Cup final, where they lost to Chicago in six games. Giroux has since established himself as a guy who can do it all, playing a hard-nosed game at either center or wing, with a devastating ability to find open teammates, while still demonstrating a knack for burying goals himself.

Because Claude was small and his journey to the NHL wasn't always a straight line, his dad couldn't help but fear the ride might end prematurely.

"I was asking myself, 'When is this going to stop? At what point is he not going to be able to perform?' " Ray said.

Now that those worries have been laid to rest, Ray can relax and enjoy watching his son do what he does best, demonstrating on the biggest hockey stage the sneaky skills he honed as a youngster playing with older, stronger kids in Hearst: "I just love those saucer passes." – *Ryan Dixon*

★★★★★★★★★★★★★★★★★★★★★★★★★★★★★★★★★★

CLAUDE GIROUX'S FAVORITE [...] GROWING UP

PLAYER: STEVE YZERMAN
JERSEY: MONTREAL CANADIENS
MUSICIAN: KENNY CHESNEY
SPORT OTHER THAN HOCKEY: BASKETBALL
SCHOOL SUBJECT: PHYS-ED
JUNK FOOD: POUTINE

★★★★★★★★★★★★★★★★★★★★★★★★★★★★★★★★★★

JOHN TAVARES

NEW YORK ISLANDERS

POSITION: CENTER
DRAFTED: 1ST OVERALL IN 2009
BORN: SEPTEMBER 20, 1990 – MISSISSAUGA, ONT.
LAST DEVELOPMENTAL TEAM: LONDON KNIGHTS (OHL)

There was a time when John Tavares wasn't the most hyped player in his age group. But it was a really, really long time ago.

"I remember the first time I hit the ice," he said. "I had the double-blade skates on."

John also recalled having a stick in his hand by the time he was three or four years old and it's with a twig that the New York Islanders center has made his reputation as a young prodigy. At five years of age, John went to his first hockey camp and that's where his parents saw the passion he had for the sport.

"House league didn't start until age six in Oakville," said Barb Tavares, John's mom. "So at the end of this skate-and-drill thing, they held a mini-tournament. That was when you saw the kids who excelled and that's when we saw the aggressiveness in John. He was lifting the puck off the ice when he shot, which is tough to do at that age."

But ask another relative and he'll tell you that the love wasn't limited to the ice. One uncle, also named John Tavares, saw the fire as well.

"It was pretty much every minute in the basement," Uncle John said. "He would start crying if people didn't play with him."

Uncle John Tavares has a unique perspective on his nephew – while the younger John became a phenomenon on the ice, the elder John had already established himself as the greatest lacrosse player in modern times and the highest

114

JOHN TAVARES HAS DEALT WITH HYPE AND EXPECTATIONS FOR A LONG TIME, BUT AT LEAST HE HAS AN UNCLE WHO KNOWS WHAT HE'S GOING THROUGH.

scorer in National Lacrosse League history as a member of the Buffalo Bandits. That pro sports atmosphere came in handy for his young nephew.

"I really looked up to him," John said. "I saw his work ethic and his passion for the game...I thought he was the coolest guy in the world. I consider him to be the greatest player ever in lacrosse."

Little John served as a ball boy for the Bandits and couldn't help catching the lacrosse bug along the way. He actually played the game at a high level until he was 16 years old and credits lacrosse for helping his first love.

"It was a great opportunity for me to get away from hockey for a few months," John said.

The similarities between the two games have helped numerous NHLers over the years, from Gary Roberts and Joe Nieuwendyk to more recent players such as John and the Islanders' 2011 top pick, Ryan Strome. In John's case, the goal-scoring prowess and quick hands that come with handling a lacrosse stick have clearly helped his NHL game.

"It's in reading the play, thinking ahead," Uncle John said. "And definitely hand-eye coordination. Plus, half the game is cross-check, cross-check, so kids in lacrosse are much more advanced when it comes to taking a hit."

Which was good for John Tavares the hockey player because his advanced skills made him a target on the ice.

"I knew at 12 or 13 that things were going pretty well," he said. "I was heavily relied upon by my team."

But with great success comes jealousy and Uncle John recalls sitting in the stands, hearing the parents of John's teammates complain about their sons not getting the puck enough. Uncle John would sit with the opponents' parents instead, where the chatter was limited to praise for his nephew's advanced skills.

John was so advanced, in fact, that his foray into major junior came a year earlier than usual. In 2004-05, he eviscerated the minor hockey circuit for 91 goals and 158 points in 72 games as a member of the Toronto Marlboros. He even played 20 games of Jr. A and posted 28 points, meaning a 14-year-old was counting more than a point per game against competition as old as 20.

The Ontario League generally didn't allow 15-year-olds to join its circuit, but John's skills merited a look-see. A special panel was set up to determine if the youngster was prepared for the rigors of the OHL schedule. Clearly the hockey part wouldn't be any concern, but how would John deal with life on the road at such a young age?

"I had to meet a lot of people," he said. "They had me write a speech about why I deserved to be in the league. It was a four or five page essay."

He also met with Paul Dennis, a sports psychologist and long time Toronto Maple Leafs player development coach who also worked with Canada's world junior team. There was also a panel of experts who asked John questions, including then-head of NHL Central Scouting, Frank Bonello, and former Maple Leaf Doug Gilmour. Having 'Killer' on the panel was a particular thrill.

"It was good as a parent, because they had a process in place," Barb said. "If they saw you lacked in a certain area, they would send you back."

> "My first rookie camp in Oshawa, I was still 14. It was a lot at once. It was all new to me."
>
> **– John Tavares**

John impressed enough that the OHL decided he was in fact ready for the circuit and the process has since become known as the "John Tavares Rule." Florida Panthers pick John McFarland tried and failed to get the same exemption the year after, while in 2011, defenseman Aaron Ekblad was successful and then went first overall to the Barrie Colts in the OHL draft.

John, naturally, went No. 1 as well. His destination was Oshawa, where the Generals offered him a place to play hockey that wasn't too far from his Oakville, Ont. home – essentially Toronto and Mississauga are in between. His parents were able to attend all his home games, but he still ended up with a billet family – and he was still so young.

"My first rookie camp in Oshawa, I was still 14," John said. "It was a lot at once. It was all new to me."

And that can be tough, even for a player as advanced as John.

"In November I hit a rough patch, homesickness," he said. "It wasn't as easy as it may have been for a 16- or 17-year-old."

On the ice, however, John excelled. His 45 goals were tops on the Generals, while his 77 points ranked second. Even though Oshawa was awful that year, the team's prized phenom brought in the good headlines, as John was named major junior's rookie of the year.

The next season proved to be even more historic. John, surrounded by a little more talent and maturing in his own right, mounted a full-frontal assault on the OHL record book. He ended the 2006-07 campaign with a preposterous 72 goals in 67 games, breaking the record for tallies by a 16-year-old. The previous title-holder was none other than Wayne Gretzky, who netted 70 in 1977-78. John ended up with 134 points that season, earning him major junior player-of-the-year honors in the process.

John Tavares ended the 2006-07 campaign with a preposterous 72 goals in 67 games, breaking the record for tallies by a 16-year-old.

As his extended OHL stay neared its end, John was once again in the news when he broke the long-held record for most goals in a career, with 215. Former Ottawa 67's left winger Peter Lee set the previous mark of 213 back in 1976.

But John would not set the record in Oshawa. Though the Generals were better by Season 4, the team still wasn't a contender and it was pretty well established that John wasn't playing a fifth season of major junior. With the future in its sights and a superstar looking for a chance to play for a title, John was traded to the London Knights along with defenseman and buddy Michael Del Zotto for a package that included future New York Rangers prospect Christian Thomas and six draft picks over the next four seasons.

"It was very difficult," John recalled. "I had to make the final call. I have so much respect for (Generals GM) Chris DePiero. We were having a fairly good season, but the opportunity in London was a significant one."

And though he finished his career in London, there's no mistaking where John's heart lies.

"I still feel that I was an Oshawa General," he said.

Thanks to his late September birthday, John had to wait a year longer to be eligible for the NHL draft. His time finally came in 2009 and the expectations were very high – as in, Sidney-Crosby high. But because he had been in the spotlight for so long, pundits and scouts began to poke holes in John's game and as things went down to the wire, some were even saying fellow OHLer Matt Duchene might be the No. 1 pick. In the end, however, the New York Islanders made the choice that had been expected for years, tabbing John with the first overall selection.

"Four years in junior was a lot of fun," John said. "But there was a lot of hype and media, so it was great to have it finally happen."

That night, after a whirlwind of activity, John and his family and friends had a post-draft party to celebrate his momentous achievement.

"I was so tired," he confessed. "I left 10 minutes in to it."

Turns out, it's never been about the parties for John.

"John was very quiet," Barb said. "He would sit back and watch before moving forward. But when he did, watch out..."

The NHL is already learning that lesson. – *Ryan Kennedy*

✶✶✶✶✶✶✶✶✶✶✶✶✶✶✶✶✶✶✶✶✶✶✶✶✶✶✶✶✶✶✶✶✶✶

JOHN TAVARES' FAVORITE [...] GROWING UP

JERSEY: TEAM CANADA
MEMORABILIA: PUCKS SIGNED BY GORDIE HOWE, BOBBY HULL AND ROCKET RICHARD
CARTOON: SCOOBY-DOO OR LOONIE TUNES
BAND: GREAT BIG SEA
MOVIE: ANCHORMAN
VIDEO GAME: EA SPORTS NHL SERIES
SCHOOL SUBJECTS: GEOGRAPHY AND MATH
JUNK FOODS: COOKIES AND CHOCOLATE CAKE

✶✶✶✶✶✶✶✶✶✶✶✶✶✶✶✶✶✶✶✶✶✶✶✶✶✶✶✶✶✶✶✶✶✶

ERIK KARLSSON

OTTAWA SENATORS

POSITION: DEFENSE
DRAFTED: 15TH OVERALL IN 2008
BORN: MAY 31, 1990 – LANDSBRO, SWEDEN
LAST DEVELOPMENTAL TEAM: FROLUNDA INDIANS (SWEDEN)

As the Ottawa Senators brass sat at the table at the 2008 NHL draft, the hometown crowd at Scotiabank Place was waiting with anticipation for them to make a selection. There was wide-ranging discussion taking place at the table.

Senators GM Bryan Murray – flanked by assistant GM Tim Murray and director of player personnel, Pierre Dorion – was getting pushed by his two top scouts to make a move from the No. 18 slot to get defenseman Erik Karlsson.

If the Senators didn't make a move to get the skilled blueliner, then somebody else would before Ottawa had a chance. The Anaheim Ducks had the No. 17 selection and the Senators were certain Erik would be snapped up.

So, Murray got on the phone.

He convinced Nashville GM David Poile to swap the 15th pick for Ottawa's No. 18 and a third-rounder in 2009 and the Senators had their man. As the trade was announced, the packed house cheered before Murray and Co. made Ottawa's pick.

The selection: defenseman Erik Karlsson from the Frolunda Indians.

"Bryan Murray said to me 'we just moved up to take a (5-foot-11) defenseman,' " Dorion said. "I said at the time, 'It's OK, Bryan, in three years you're going to love him.' It's three years later and he loves him."

Anybody who has watched Erik play can't help but notice his talent. He hasn't got the size, but he's got speed and the skills to pay the bills.

Erik, who turned 21 in May of 2011, has wanted to be a hockey player since he first laced up his skates back in Landsbro, Sweden as a three-year-old. His desire was always to be the best and he never let his modest size get in the way.

"I almost had skates on from the time I was able to walk," Erik said. "It was just something I loved to do from the time I was a kid. I just always wanted to be a hockey player.

"There wasn't a lot to do in the wintertime in Sweden. If you wanted to be outside, you wanted to be outside playing hockey. That's how I got into it."

Like a lot of kids, Erik wanted to be a goalie – for a while.

"When I was a kid, my dad took a slapshot at me and I started crying," he said. "I've never been a goalie since."

That's good news for the Senators. In addition to firing the odd puck at him, father Jonas Karlsson also instilled a strong work ethic in his son. Jonas was a lumberjack and Erik's first job was working in his father's shop. The tasks were tough, but young Erik learned what hard work can accomplish.

Growing up, Erik also spent a lot of time with his father at the rink, where his dad served as his coach. There were some tense moments, so the father-son duo had to learn how to balance their relationship. But ultimately, it brought them closer.

"He coached me until I was 13 years old, then he told me he couldn't help me anymore," Erik said. "Hockey was always something that we did. There were some silent car rides home, that's for sure. But, he did a good job.

"As my coach, he did a good job by not giving me special treatment and he wasn't too hard on me, either just because I was his son. When you spend so much time together – on and off the ice – there was pretty much something that happened in every practice or every game."

> **"I almost had skates on from the time I was able to walk. I just always wanted to be a hockey player."**
>
> **– Erik Karlsson**

When it was time for Erik to move on to more competitive hockey, Jonas stepped down from his duties as coach.

"He just felt that it was time for somebody else to start coaching me," Erik said. "I think he felt (at 13) I could make my own decisions (about hockey). He didn't feel I needed to ask him all the time about what I needed to do.

"He just wanted me to be on my own in that age group. He wanted me to make my own decisions and learn from my own mistakes. He felt like if he stopped me sometimes he was just going to be in the way."

Just six years later, Erik played in his first NHL game. On Oct. 3, 2009 at the age of 19, he suited up against the New York Rangers. He even got an assist.

Not only has Erik provided an injection of youth to the Senators dressing room, he has also brought a sense of humor. After being selected for the 2011 All-Star Game, Erik let it slip that he wasn't exactly a model student in school.

Asked by reporters if he'd been sent to the principal's office, Erik shot back, "A lot of times."

Of course, it wasn't anything too offensive.

"I never got expelled or anything like that," he said. "Things you did when you were a kid. Did some pranks on other kids or the teachers, maybe. Sometimes you'd miss a class...just small things like that."

Being selected to play in the All-Star Game certainly hasn't caused Erik to rest on his laurels. His 13 goals and 45 points in 75 games as a sophomore during the 2010-11 campaign were great totals, but only represent the tip of the iceberg in terms of where he wants to go. And Erik knows what it takes to get there.

"There's always work here if you want to stay in the NHL because everybody gets better around you," he said. "You can't forget what it took you to get here and you have to make sure that you keep working."

The transition to North America has been made easier by the fact Erik has a good mentor in the dressing room in the form of captain Daniel Alfredsson. Coincidentally, it was Alfredsson who announced Erik's selection at the entry draft on behalf of the Senators on that warm June night in Ottawa.

FROM LANDSBRO, SWEDEN TO OTTAWA, ONT., ERIK KARLSSON LEADS A BATCH OF PROMISING YOUNGSTERS WHO ARE LOOKING TO GET THE SENATORS BACK WITH THE EAST'S ELITE.

Not wanting an 18-year-old living in a hotel room or living on his own for that matter, Alfredsson gave Erik a warm place to stay during training camp. Alfredsson's wife, Bibi Bachman, didn't mind one bit and his three kids were happy because they had someone to play video games with.

Heck, Erik even got the odd babysitting shift. But it's in the dressing room, on the ice and in the gym where Alfredsson has influenced Erik the most. The pair even spend their off-seasons together in Gothenburg, Sweden.

"As far as my playing, he has been a big supporter for me," Erik said. "Even if he's not going to be (playing) for much longer, I think he has done so much for me already. We've spent so much time together."

It might seem odd that a player in the twilight of his career and young guy just learning the ropes could have such a special bond, but Erik and Alfredsson definitely share a kinship.

When Alfredsson competed for Sweden at the Olympics in Vancouver, he brought Erik back a special present: A stick from legendary Detroit Red Wings defenseman Nicklas Lidstrom, one of Erik's heroes when he was growing up. It was just more evidence of the bond shared between 'Alfie' and Erik.

> **"I don't really know where I'd be without Daniel Alfredsson. It's as simple as that."**
>
> **– Erik Karlsson**

"I got to know (Alfredsson) before I got to Ottawa and once I got there he helped me out to reach that next level," Erik said. "He is still helping me to move forward in my career.

"I don't really know where I'd be without him. It's as simple as that."

Erik said he hasn't reached his potential as a player. It's been quite a journey, from skating on a frozen pond in Sweden, to being selected by the team hosting the draft in '08, to now lifting Sens fans out of their seats in that same arena. Suffice it to say, the last few years have been a whirlwind.

"Everything seems like it has happened pretty fast," Erik said. "I'm just going to keep working hard to be a better player. As a player, I'm not happy with where I am today. Maybe I should be, but I think you can always get better."
– *Bruce Garrioch*

★★★★★★★★★★★★★★★★★★★★★★★★★★★★★★★★★★★★

ERIK KARLSSON'S FAVORITE [...] GROWING UP

PLAYERS: DANIEL ALFREDSSON OR PETER FORSBERG
JERSEY: DETROIT RED WINGS
MEMORABILIA: NICK LIDSTROM'S STICK OR DANIEL ALFREDSSON'S GLOVES FROM THE OLYMPICS
CARTOON: DONALD DUCK
VIDEO GAME: CALL OF DUTY
SPORT OTHER THAN HOCKEY: SOCCER
SCHOOL SUBJECT: ENGLISH
JUNK FOOD: PIZZA

★★★★★★★★★★★★★★★★★★★★★★★★★★★★★★★★★★★★

JOHN CARLSON

POSITION: DEFENSE

DRAFTED: 27TH OVERALL IN 2008

BORN: JANUARY 10, 1990 – NATICK, MA.

LAST DEVELOPMENTAL TEAM: LONDON KNIGHTS (OHL)

When it comes to post-game analysis, not many TV studios can hold a candle to the conversations that take place during the drive home from a youth hockey contest.

In the confines of the family car, the preceding events are often dissected in detail, the components of a big win fondly re-lived or in the case of a loss, the time is spent sorting out where it all went wrong.

While headlights were guiding Dick Carlson and his talented son, John, home, the man in the driver's seat often found himself a bit flabbergasted by how the kid beside him could make peace with a bad game by the time he slammed the passenger-side door shut. Dick was a college-level defenseman in his day and, as the coach of John's New Jersey Rockets AAA team, he took the outcomes of games very seriously. That's why it would sometimes drive him a bit nuts when his son was able to shake things off so easily.

Dick relayed the message he would often get from John after a tough loss: "Dad, we have another game tomorrow. I'll be better tomorrow, don't worry about it."

John's ability to put things behind him wasn't a result of not caring about the game, he was as invested as anybody. It was, however, an indication of an emerging personality trait that still serves him well to this day.

"Clearly, most of the guys who make it, have that attitude," Dick said. "They don't want it to carry through two, three, four games in a row, but they realize there are ups and downs and you've got to put it behind you as fast as you can."

CAPITALS DEFENSEMAN JOHN CARLSON BROKE THE HEARTS OF CANADIAN HOCKEY FANS WITH HIS OT GOAL IN THE FINAL OF 2010 WORLD JUNIOR CHAMPIONSHIP, BUT HE'S GRABBED THE HEARTS OF FANS IN WASHINGTON WITH HIS SIZE AND SKILL.

Remaining on an even keel may have come naturally to John, but some lessons that ultimately served him well weren't so easy to absorb initially. As John's coach for the vast majority of his youth hockey years, Dick readily admits he was harder on his son, often using John as the conduit to send a message to the entire team.

"I beat him up," Dick said. "We had an agreement where I said, 'Look, John, you're going to be the example. You're not going to like it, but that's the way it's gotta be.'

"There were days he understood it and days he didn't understand it. And it wasn't always fair to him, either."

That may be so, but Dick said it helped condition John for the criticism every pro athlete faces at some point. And Dick also gave John a ton of credit for his ability to take tough love in stride, in large part because he simply loved playing the game.

That passion first sprung up while the Carlson family was living in the Boston area, where John was born and Dick, who played Div. III hockey with Framingham State, gained his love of the sport while watching Bobby Orr and the Bruins. But everybody's hockey adoration was put to the test when the family moved to New Jersey when John was about five years old. Suffice it to say, whacking a puck around was not among the more common things to do in John's new surroundings.

"In the town we lived in, Colonia, hockey was not big at all," John said. "I think there was only one other kid who played at any level at all."

Through his old contacts in Massachusetts, Dick found out about the Rockets program, which was run out of nearby Bridgewater. Along with Andrew, his older brother by two years, John began playing for the Rockets and his skills soon became apparent. (Andrew also had a knack for the game and went on to face Philadelphia Flyers star James van Riemsdyk as a high school player.)

But while John found plenty of kids in the Bridgewater area who shared his fondness for the game, his passion for hockey was met with some blank stares when he'd return home to Colonia. Not that that was a necessarily a bad thing.

"That's all we would talk about with our friends when we were younger," John said. "I don't even know if anyone really understood too much. I think everyone thought it was cool cause it was so different."

Playing for the Rockets gave John the chance to travel all over the United States and Canada for tournaments. His most lasting memory from those days, however, happened right in his own rink when, through some connections in the Rockets program, New Jersey Devils defensemen Scott Stevens and Ken Daneyko showed up for practice. If being instructed by a big-league pair was supposed to help the kids refine their skills, the ploy backfired.

"We were all just star struck," John said. "We didn't even want to practise, were just wanted to stare at them and watch what they were doing on the ice."

It's understandable why anybody watching John play defense for the Washington Capitals these days is wowed by his ability, but despite how natural he looks back there the blueline wasn't always his domain. John started out as a forward, but made the change when he was about 13 years old because he was one of the bigger kids at the time and it was already apparent he had a terrific feel for the game.

"With his size and how he could read the play, it seemed like a natural to move him back to 'D,' " Dick said.

According to Charlie Skjodt, who coached John while he played one year with the United States League's Indiana Ice, the switch was a stroke of genius.

"It's probably the best move his dad has ever made," said Skjodt, now team president for the Ice. "He could have been a great forward, too, but he is a born defenseman in my opinion."

"John Carlson could have been a great forward, too, but he is a born defenseman in my opinion."

— Charlie Skjodt

When John moved to Indiana, he already had a scholarship offer to play NCAA hockey for the UMass Minutemen. Skjodt hadn't seen John play in person, as is the norm with teenagers who come from outside the USHL region to play in the league. It didn't take long for him to formulate an opinion.

"I knew the first day I watched him on the ice he was going to be an NHL pick," Skjodt said.

Following his year with the Ice, John was selected 27th overall by the Capitals. At that point, John decided to jump to the London Knights of the Ontario League. For a long time, John's main goal was getting an education out of hockey and with a dad who played in the NCAA and coming from a place where the college path is the standard trail, moving to Canada to play major junior was a huge decision. But the instincts that serve him so well on and off the ice kicked in and John made his call.

John Carlson has gained a reputation as a winner, thanks to the fact he claimed back-to-back Calder Cups in the American League and a gold medal at the 2010 world juniors.

"It was all feel for him," Dick said. "It was, 'Dad, I'm ready to go.' And there was no second-guessing."

The decision clearly paid off as John has become one of the most highly regarded young reorguards in the game. He's also gained a reputation as a winner, thanks to the fact he claimed back-to-back Calder Cups in the American League with the Hershey Bears. There's also the small matter of John scoring the overtime winner for Team USA as it defeated Canada in its own backyard during the 2010 World Junior Championship gold medal showdown in Saskatoon, Sask.

"It was kind of a blur how it all panned out," John said. "It felt like they were almost scoring on us and the next thing you know I had the puck on my stick and we were on a 2-on-1."

The last few years in general have been a whirlwind for John as he started the hockey season in different cities for four consecutive campaigns, culminating with his stellar rookie campaign with the Caps in 2010-11.

"It's been a crazy few years," John said. "This has developed so quickly I really didn't get a chance to look back and see how it all happened.

"It kept me on my toes and I really enjoyed each place I went to a lot. Every team that I was on was also at the top of the league every year and in the hunt to win."

Now that he's found a permanent home in Washington, you can bet John will stay true to that levelheaded kid who was always able to shrug off the bad days and focus on what's ahead.

"That's John," Dick said. "To this day he goes to the rink with a smile on his face. He's doing what he wants to do."
— *Ryan Dixon*

★★★★★★★★★★★★★★★★★★★★★★★★★★★★★★★★★★★

JOHN CARLSON'S FAVORITE [...] GROWING UP

PLAYER: SCOTT STEVENS
JERSEY: QUEBEC NORDIQUES (JOE SAKIC)
VIDEO GAME: EA SPORTS NHL SERIES
BAND: O.A.R.
SPORT OTHER THAN HOCKEY: LACROSSE
SUBJECT: MATH
JUNK FOOD: ICE CREAM

★★★★★★★★★★★★★★★★★★★★★★★★★★★★★★★★★★★

EVANDER KANE

WINNIPEG JETS

POSITION: LEFT WING
DRAFTED: 4TH OVERALL IN 2009
BORN: AUGUST 2, 1991 – VANCOUVER, B.C.
LAST DEVELOPMENTAL TEAM: VANCOUVER GIANTS (WHL)

Evander Kane has made some pretty impressive leaps in his hockey career, but he was going in circles for a while.

Unlike the majority of NHLers, Evander did not begin playing organized hockey around the same time he entered Kindergarten. His dad, Perry Kane, preferred to work 1-on-1 with Evander so the youngster's fundamentals would be well refined before he joined a team. When Evander was about six years old, Perry took him to a parents and tots skate at a local rink near their Vancouver home.

"I had him out there to skate the circles and another parent started talking to me and we're having this conversation," Perry recalled. "The whole time we were talking Evander was still skating the circle. I said, 'OK, sorry son, you can stop now!' "

Perry's plan to more thoroughly develop and expand Evander's skill set before putting him in youth hockey wasn't always a hit with his son, who, naturally, saw the fun other kids his age were having playing on teams. Beyond a desire to mold Evander into a player who could handle all the basics, Perry understood the all-encompassing commitment that playing on a club can be and with two other young children, daughters Brea and Kyla, on the scene, he wasn't sure there was enough time to be running around town to rinks.

Perry likely knew the time management argument would be a tough sell on his anxious son, so instead he kept setting ever-raising standards for Evander to reach, taking an, "As soon as you can do this, then you can play" approach.

"Then he would fall down and I would say, 'See, you can't do it yet,' " Perry chuckled.

But Evander got the last laugh when, like all sensible kids, he took his case to a higher court.

"He wanted to put me in hockey when I was 10," Evander said of his dad's plan. "I wanted to play and my mom actually went and signed me up when I was eight, so I thank her for that."

Evander eventually found himself playing for Vancouver's North Shore Winter Club, where he caught the eye of his hometown Western League team, the Vancouver Giants. When the Giants decided to take Evander 19th overall in the 2006 WHL bantam draft, Perry was over the moon.

"I couldn't have scripted it any better," he said. "You get to play for the Giants, your hometown (team), and you get to be coached by Don Hay, who I considered the best coach in the league."

Yet another bonus to being selected by the Giants was that they were slated to host the next Memorial Cup. But with Evander set to play a season of minor midget with the Vancouver Canadians, a major junior championship seemed like a very distant, unrealistic goal until he had a pep talk with Perry.

> "My dad wanted to put me in hockey when I was 10. I wanted to play and my mom actually went and signed me up when I was eight, so I thank her for that."
>
> **— Evander Kane**

"My dad came in, I remember him mentioning to me that they were hosting the Memorial Cup," Evander recalled. "He said, 'You better start working hard,' and luckily enough I was able to make my way up there and play with them in the playoffs and then win the Memorial Cup. That was a pretty good start to my WHL career."

The next season, his first full 'Dub' campaign, Evander earned a nomination for rookie of the year thanks to 24 goals and 41 points in 65 games. Then, in the year he became draft-eligible for the NHL, Evander exploded with 48 goals and 96 points in 61 games, good for fourth in league scoring. That December, he was invited to try out for Canada's 2009 World Junior Championship entry.

Considered a bit of a long shot to make the team, Evander impressed at camp and felt pretty good about his chances after playing two quality exhibition games. On the eve of the final cuts, Evander, like many Canadians, tuned into TSN and watched as analysts Gord Miller and Pierre McGuire selected him to their tournament roster. Unfortunately, Canadian coach Pat Quinn arrived at a different conclusion on the 17-year-old.

"I had never been cut before so it was obviously disappointing," Evander said. "With the world juniors, you never know if you're going to be able to play in that again."

As it turned out, his world juniors experience mirrored his early days in youth hockey; he was eventually going to get on the team, he just had to endure a waiting period. The sting of being left off the squad was healed when center Dana Tyrell injured his knee in a pre-tournament game versus Sweden. Evander got the call and quickly showed he belonged all along. He started the tournament as Canada's 13th forward, but jumped up the depth chart by exceeding expectations in every role. By the end of the event, Evander had two goals and six points in six games for the gold medal-winning Canadians.

Hay, who coached Evander for three years in the WHL, said that showing exemplified the drive and belief in his own abilities that Evander possesses.

"He has the confidence in himself to play in pressure situations and perform well," Hay said.

The Atlanta Thrashers obviously agreed, taking him with their first pick – fourth overall – at the 2009 draft. Evander attended the Thrashers training camp the following fall and demonstrated enough upside to crack the lineup as an 18-year-old. Part of the reason he was able to make the huge leap to the big show was because he knows how to handle himself physically. Evander definitely benefits from his 6-foot-2, 195-pound frame, but he also has the advantage of some exposure to boxing, a sport Perry loves. In fact, Evander is named after former heavyweight champion Evander Holyfield.

"I really liked his toughness, the fact he could take a shot and keep on going," Perry said of Holyfield.

EVANDER KANE GOT
HIS NAME FROM HIS
FATHER'S LOVE OF
BOXING, BUT THE
YOUNGSTER HAS MADE
A NAME FOR HIMSELF
MOSTLY WITH HIS
SCORING PROWESS.

Perry also knew from experience that if his son was going to play high-level hockey, he had to learn to protect himself. Evander may have had to wait until he was eight to play hockey, but Perry, growing up in the predominantly black community of East Preston, N.S., didn't put blade to ice in a rink until he was 13.

Clearly a quick study, Perry began playing for an all-black team, went on to play high school hockey and, eventually skated for St. Francis Xavier University in Antigonish, N.S. Perry carved out enough of a reputation for himself that Evander says he still has senior members of NHL organizations approach him on occasion and ask, "Are you Perry Kane's son?"

Though he had obvious hockey skill, Perry claims he would have been a boxer if not for his dad, who did fight in the ring, turning away all the trainers who came to the family house because he didn't want his son following in his footsteps. Perry's cousin, Kirk Johnson, did put the gloves on and represented Canada at the 1992 Summer Olympics in Barcelona, Spain.

When Perry moved west to and started a family in Vancouver, he carried his two sporting loves with him, putting Evander in the boxing gym to train and learn some fighting techniques when he was about 13. His intention wasn't to turn his son into an on-ice knuckle-chucker, but rather to make sure he knew how to properly throw a punch for the inevitable moments when he would have to protect himself. Now, Evander uses boxing practices to maintain his impressive physique.

> **His willingness to cut hard to the net and always try to get shots on goal should make Evander Kane an instant Manitoba fan favorite.**

"Boxing is just for conditioning, it's a great workout," he said.

Evander has progressed well his first two seasons in the NHL, recording 26 points in 66 games as a freshman in 2009-10, then jumping to 19 goals and 43 points in 73 games as a second-year player. With the Thrashers now based in Winnipeg, the 20-year-old Evander is right on target to become a focal point in the franchise for years to come.

136

His willingness to cut hard to the net and always try to get shots on goal should make him an instant Manitoba fan favorite. No doubt they'll see the same passion Perry witnessed when he finally remembered to look over to the big faceoff circle way back when and saw his kid burning around the ice.

"I thought then there was a chance he could do well in hockey because he was a good student and he obviously loved the game, so that made it easy," Perry said.

And whenever the hard stuff came along, Evander was more than capable of handling it.

"He'll give and take," Perry said. "He's not a dirty player, that's fine, just take your number and go from there." – *Ryan Dixon*

★★★★★★★★★★★★★★★★★★★★★★★★★★★★★★★★★★★★★

EVANDER KANE'S FAVORITE [...] GROWING UP

PLAYERS: JOE SAKIC AND JAROME IGINLA
JERSEY: MIGHTY DUCKS OF ANAHEIM (TEEMU SELANNE)
ARTIST: LIL WAYNE
MOVIE: DUMB AND DUMBER
VIDEO GAME: EA SPORTS NHL SERIES
SPORT OTHER THAN HOCKEY: SOCCER
FAVORITE SUBJECT: SCIENCE
JUNK FOOD: PIZZA

★★★★★★★★★★★★★★★★★★★★★★★★★★★★★★★★★★★★

137

CAM FOWLER

POSITION: DEFENSE
DRAFTED: 12TH OVERALL IN 2010
BORN: DECEMBER 5, 1991 – WINDSOR, ONT.
LAST DEVELOPMENTAL TEAM: WINDSOR SPITFIRES (OHL)

Every hockey player dreams of getting to the NHL someday, but that doesn't mean there aren't other aspirations that have to fall by the wayside. For Anaheim defenseman Cam Fowler, he always takes a pause when he thinks about baseball.

"I still miss it to this day," he said. "It's hard to pass by a diamond."

Growing up in Farmington Hills, Mich., Cam excelled at both sports and played baseball up until he left to play for the U.S. national team development program in nearby Ann Arbor.

"Farmington is my home and I'm always going to come back here," Cam said. "I really got to do everything a kid likes to do. I got to mess around with a lot of sports."

As a baseball player, Cam helped his high school team all the way to the state final and played travel baseball for as long as he had played travel hockey. And while the summer game was a passion, his parents originally got him into the sport so he would have something different from hockey during the warmer months.

"At the end of the hockey season, I wanted him to take off his skates and try something else," said Cam's dad, Perry Fowler.

Born in Canada, Perry naturally had a love for hockey and gave his son every opportunity to enjoy the iced game as well. Fortunately for Perry, Cam fell in love, too.

"I remember just looking at pictures of hockey," Cam reminisced. "My parents said I always had a stick in my hand and I'd be whacking a ball around the house, making a mess."

The family would go public skating on Sunday afternoons and Cam was on the ice before his fourth birthday. By age six he was playing travel hockey and by eight he was a member of Honeybaked, one of the top programs in the area, along with teams like Little Caesar's and Compuware. Cam enjoyed having baseball as a counterbalance during those years.

"It's definitely different from hockey," he said. "Baseball is more based on individual stats."

But as an individual, Cam was pretty special as well. So if any kid was going to get college recruitment offers way before he was eligible to attend an institute of higher learning, it was Cam.

"He was a freshman in high school," Perry recalled. "After Spring Break he started getting offers. At the time it seemed like the path he was going to take. He could play hockey and get a free education; what could be better than that?"

> "I still miss baseball to this day. It's hard to pass by a diamond."
>
> **– Cam Fowler**

As nice as the attention was, it was also pretty daunting for a 14-year-old to be weighing the merits of which university he would attend when he had really only begun taking high school classes. Perry said he had to make an Excel spreadsheet at work in order to keep track of all the schools interested in his son.

"It was really an overwhelming experience," Cam said. "If I didn't have my family and my agents there, it would have been tough. But I think that's how the game is going these days. You need all the info."

Cam was known for his tremendous skating and puckhandling abilities from the blueline and that made him one of the more prominent members of the U.S. NTDP just as the program was hitting a new gear. And while Cam was practically a local, some of his teammates were coming from Alaska or Texas, so his time in Ann Arbor became a continental learning experience.

CAM FOWLER WAS SLOTTED TO BE A TOP-FIVE DRAFT PICK, BUT ENDED UP SLIPPING TO THE MIDDLE OF THE ROUND, WHERE THE ANAHEIM DUCKS WERE MORE THAN HAPPY TO SNAP HIM UP.

It was also a crash-course in success. Along with top NHL prospects such as Jeremy Morin, Danny Kristo and Jerry D'Amigo, Cam helped the Red, White and Blue to several big milestones, including gold at the under-18s and a dramatic victory over Canada to win the 2010 World Junior Championship in Saskatoon, Sask.

But by the time Cam and his American brethren were celebrating their upset on Canadian ice, the kid from Michigan had already made another life-altering choice.

Before the 2009-10 season began, Cam decided not to go the college route after all. Instead he was scooped up by the Ontario League powerhouse Windsor Spitfires, a team that had won the Memorial Cup the year before and featured the No. 1 prospect for the 2010 draft, winger Taylor Hall.

There was controversy about the signing at the time, particularly from people who felt Cam had broken his commitment to Notre Dame, the school he ultimately had signed a letter of intent with.

But Perry maintains that his son was very up front with his suitors. Cam told Notre Dame he would sign the letter of intent, but that his final decision on whether he would play college hockey or major junior had not yet been established. The Spitfires were told the same thing.

The longer junior schedule and a chance to play on the best team in Canada won out in the end and once again Cam was just a quick drive from home. Whether geography was a factor or not, Cam was excellent with the Spitfires, scoring at a point-per-game rate during the regular season, winning the previously mentioned gold medal at the world juniors in the middle, then helping Windsor to its second straight OHL crown before heading off to another Memorial Cup. For an American kid, the legendary tournament featuring the OHL, Quebec League and Western League champs plus a host team, was a bit of a mystery.

"Growing up in Michigan, I didn't have an understanding of the Memorial Cup," Cam said. "But it's a grind and I think it helped prepare me for the NHL."

Windsor cruised over the host Brandon Wheat Kings 9-1 in the tourney's final and the big leagues were next on Cam's agenda. Heading into the draft, Cam had been regularly slotted at third or fourth overall. His teammate, Hall, was a near consensus No. 1, while fellow OHLer Tyler Seguin was the stalking horse at No. 2. Another OHLer, Kingston defenseman Erik Gudbranson, was also in the mix.

The family headed to Los Angeles for the draft and after a party at his agency's headquarters on the Thursday, everything was set up for a magical Friday. But the draft is a fickle beast and things don't always turn out the way people think.

True, Hall went first, followed by Seguin. Then Gudbranson was taken by Florida. Columbus went off the board by selecting center Ryan Johansen next and all of a sudden Cam's stock was sliding.

"Being a hockey fan, I know things don't always work out the way you expect them to," Perry said.

He had done his own mock draft and knew that with Columbus drafting fleet-footed blueliner John Moore the year before, the Blue Jackets were unlikely to tab his similarly skilled son. As the picks went on, Cam began to feel the heat and when the New York Rangers grabbed bruising defenseman Dylan McIlrath with the 10th pick, the crowd and media really started to hone in on Cam.

"Sitting by him was tough," Perry said. "His heart was beating fast. The camera was in his face the entire time. I mean, the *entire* time."

Eventually, Anaheim snapped up Cam with the 12th pick overall and he was greeted onstage by future Hall of Famer Scott Niedermayer, a pretty good skater from the back end in his own right. Thanks to his buzz coming into the draft, Cam got to go to the Stanley Cup final and be interviewed by Don Cherry, as well as take part in the pre-draft luncheon. All signs had pointed to him being top-five. When that didn't happen, Cam at least found the silver lining.

"I tried to hide my disappointment and the emotions on my face, but it still hurts to watch it," he said. "But at the end of the day, I was still a first round draft pick."

And one that paid dividends right away. The Ducks came into the 2010-11 season with a drastically revamped defense corps, one that had lost Niedermayer and Aaron Ward to retirement, as well as veteran James

> "Sitting by Cam at the draft was tough. His heart was beating fast. The camera was in his face the entire time. I mean, the entire time."
>
> **– Perry Fowler**

Wisniewski to free agency. New recruit Toni Lydman was hurt at the beginning of the season and the blueline was pilloried by opponents before righting itself.

Cam had impressed in training camp and made the team thanks to his skill game. He stuck around for the whole campaign, logging an impressive 22:07 of average ice time, placing him third among NHL rookies and fifth on the Ducks.

"Seven or eight games in, I realized people had accepted me," Cam said. "They thought I could play and make a difference. I'm so happy to be a Duck."

Cam cited Paul Mara as one Anaheim blueliner who truly took him under his wing and the kid even got in on some opening night fun when he drove Teemu Selanne to the Honda Center in the Finn's ultra-expensive Maybach luxury car – wearing a chauffeur's outfit, of course.

But Cam's no longer a rookie and as the years go by, his role on the Ducks will continue to grow. Though there were speed bumps along the way, he's precisely where he wanted to be all along. – *Ryan Kennedy*

★★★★★★★★★★★★★★★★★★★★★★★★★★★★★★★★★★

CAM FOWLER'S FAVORITE [...] GROWING UP

PLAYER: NICKLAS LIDSTROM
JERSEY: PITTSBURGH PENGUINS
MEMORABILIA: WORLD JUNIORS STICK SIGNED BY ALL HIS TEAMMATES
CARTOON: ROCKET POWER
ALBUM: THA CARTER III BY LIL WAYNE OR GRADUATION BY KANYE WEST
MOVIE: TOMMY BOY
SPORTS OTHER THAN HOCKEY: GOLF AND BASEBALL
SCHOOL SUBJECT: HISTORY
JUNK FOOD: POTATO CHIPS

★★★★★★★★★★★★★★★★★★★★★★★★★★★★★★★★★★

JORDAN EBERLE

POSITION: RIGHT WING
DRAFTED: 22ND OVERALL IN 2008
BORN: MAY 15, 1990 – REGINA, SASK.
LAST DEVELOPMENTAL TEAM: REGINA PATS (WHL)

The word "big" has followed Jordan Eberle around his entire hockey life, albeit in vastly different contexts. For much of his career, Jordan was forced to hear over and over how he wasn't big enough to make it as a hockey player. But by the end of his time in major junior, he'd carved out a reputation as a big-game player few, if any, could match.

As a youngster growing up in Regina, Sask., Jordan likely would have been drawn to hockey even if his older cousin, Derek Eberle, wasn't playing defense for the hometown Pats in the Western League.

Jordan and his three siblings are just five years apart in total, so hockey games were common in and around the Eberle household. Jordan has two older sisters and the eldest, Whitney, played the game at a competitive level before eventually moving on to other interests. Jordan's younger brother, Dustin, has spent time playing Jr. A in the Saskatchewan League.

Like most kids who eventually go on to make the NHL, it was obvious early on that Jordan had an aptitude for the game.

"He was always one of the best players around," said his father, Darren Eberle.

That first became apparent when Jordan participated in the renowned Brick AAA novice tournament in Edmonton. After being passed over by the team representing his home province, Jordan was approached to join a club from Vancouver called the Vipers. He made the trip west and his

Vancouver club ended up beating a Toronto-based team featuring Steven Stamkos in the final and Jordan was named tournament MVP.

At that point, a deep-pocketed AAA organization called the Boston Icemen invited a few Canadian kids such as Jordan, Stamkos and future New York Islanders defenseman Travis Hamonic to join their outfit, travelling to events throughout the summer all over North America.

"They would start to contact me and fly us into tournaments, whether it was Toronto, Quebec, Detroit," Darren said.

JORDAN EBERLE MAY BE SHORT IN STATURE, BUT FEW IN THE HOCKEY WORLD DISPLAY MORE HEART ON A NIGHTLY BASIS. SOMETHING OILERS FANS ARE LEARNING EACH SEASON.

Believe it or not, being carted around the country to play in these big tournaments for a couple summers before he was even a teenager didn't really register as something all that unique to Jordan.

"I didn't think too much of it at the time," he said. "It was more just playing hockey and a team wants you to play for them. I remember with the talent we had on the team we used to just go to tournaments and whup everyone's butts."

Jordan and Stamkos often played on a line together and would just devastate the competition.

"We'd go to tournaments and it was almost like we'd rotate; one of us would be the MVP, the other would be the top scorer," Jordan said with a chuckle. "It would just go back and forth."

Though Jordan's talents were obvious, his slight size wasn't doing him any favors in the eyes of scouts, especially those bird-dogging for Western League clubs on the hunt for kids to play in the toughest major junior circuit in Canada.

Jordan spent the 2004-05 season as a member of the prominent Notre Dame Hounds high school program in Wilcox, Sask. That summer, he was selected by his hometown Pats in the WHL bantam draft, but not until the seventh round.

Size, again, was the knock against Jordan. Regina held the first pick in that draft and took blueliner Colten Teubert, who was already listed at 6-foot-4. That meant he had about a full foot on Jordan, who was easily one of the smallest players in the 'Dub' draft.

By this point the Eberles had moved to Calgary and, in 2005-06, Jordan and goalie Jacob DeSerres – who went on to win the Memorial Cup with the Saint John Sea Dogs in 2011 – were the only two 15-year-olds selected to play midget AAA hockey with the Calgary Buffaloes. Jordan asserted himself well, netting 34 points in 31 games. The Buffaloes went all the way to the Telus Cup final, losing the national title in triple-overtime to the Prince Albert Mintos. It was during that campaign Darren began noticing Jordan wasn't going to let himself get pushed around, regardless of size discrepancies.

"I could see, even in midget AAA at 15 playing against 16- and 17-year-olds, he was starting to show more greasiness and ability to fend off bigger guys in the corners," he said, "kind of learning his craft based on smarts and maneuverability."

At that point, Darren still thought Jordan would likely end up going the NCAA route, which tends to be kinder to small players. In the fall of 2006, Jordan earned a spot with the Alberta Junior League's Okotoks Oilers, who played about 15 minutes from the Eberle home south of Calgary.

With a Jr. A spot already in his back pocket, Jordan headed to Regina for Pats camp. His strong showing there proved he not only belonged, but had a chance to excel, which prompted Darren to ask the Pats coach a blunt question.

"I said, 'If he shows he can play as a top-six or one of your top guys, do you have any issue playing him as a 16-year-old?' " Darren said. "Curtis Hunt squarely said 'No.' "

Still, the decision facing Jordan was a big one. If he played just one exhibition game with the Pats, he would burn his NCAA eligibility. After having a pow wow with the Regina brass, Darren sat in a room alone with his son and asked him if, considering all that was at stake, he was sure he wanted to play in the WHL. The answer came back affirmative.

"I grew up watching the Pats and always dreamt of playing there," Jordan said. "So when I got the opportunity I took it."

And took full advantage of it. Billeting with his grandparents and playing in front of family and friends, Jordan led the Pats with 28 goals as a rookie and the following season, he paced Regina with 42 goals and 75 points in 70 contests. Proving the people who claimed he'd never be able to play in the WHL wrong provided a chip of some size on Jordan's shoulder, but he said the greater goal and source of motivation was to be drafted by an NHL team.

In June of 2008, the right winger went from a seventh round WHL pick to a first round NHL selection when the Edmonton Oilers nabbed him 22nd overall.

> "I grew up watching the Regina Pats and always dreamt of playing there. So when I got the opportunity I took it."
>
> — **Jordan Eberle**

As a first-rounder picked by a Canadian team, Jordan was a known commodity in the hockey community at that point. But between draft day and making the Oilers two years later, Jordan's heroics at consecutive World Junior Championships carved him out a national profile it's fair to say nobody saw coming – especially after he did nothing to distinguish himself positively at the team's summer gathering in 2008.

> ## "The building just went boom! I'd never experienced that kind of noise or excitement."
> ## – Darren Eberle

"I had a really bad camp, I was maybe the worst player there," Jordan said with a laugh, adding he didn't even expect to be invited to the winter camp.

But the call came and Jordan got himself on the squad for the 2009 WJC in Ottawa. He found his niche playing on a line with Zach Boychuk and center Cody Hodgson. As usual, Canada was expected to win gold – especially on home ice – but in the dying seconds of their semifinal game versus Russia, the Canadians trailed 5-4.

Having scored once already in the game, Jordan parked himself in front of Russian goalie Vadim Zhelobnyuk and, after a great play by teammate Ryan Ellis to keep the puck in at the blueline, Jordan found himself alone on the lip of the crease with the biscuit on his blade. He made a quick move to his backhand and shoveled the puck past Zhelobnyuk to knot the game with five seconds remaining on the clock.

"The building just went 'boom!' " said Darren, who was in attendance as part of a big family contingent. "I'd never experienced that kind of noise or excitement."

After overtime settled nothing, Jordan helped Canada advance in the shootout by scoring again to complete an unofficial hat trick. In the final contest, Canada trounced Sweden 5-1 to claim its fifth consecutive gold medal, with Jordan adding an empty-netter to give him six goals and 13 points in six WJC games, good for third in tournament scoring behind teammates Hodgson and John Tavares.

The following year, with the event held in his home province of Saskatchewan, Jordan further entrenched his legend when he scored twice in the final three minutes of the gold-medal game versus Team USA to send the affair to overtime. Though the Americans prevailed on John Carlson's winner, Jordan's standing as the most clutch player in WJC history was firmly established.

While Darren acknowledged nobody – not even the most optimistic father – could have anticipated heroics on that level, he did say Jordan always displayed a flair for the dramatics.

"The bigger the game, the bigger he played," he said.

Jordan chuckled when he characterized his game-tying tallies in back-to-back years at the WJC as "the two luckiest goals I've ever scored." There was little luck involved when Jordan took to the ice for his first NHL game on Oct. 7 of 2010 and scored a highlight-reel shorthanded goal against Miikka Kiprusoff and the Calgary Flames to put an exclamation point on the start of his Oilers career. What else would you expect from a guy who has always thrived in adrenaline-fuelled scenarios?

"I think everyone is like that," he said. "You get into a situation where the game is tied or you're down by one, something happens where it just sparks you and you get excited to play and you want to be the guy to score and help your team win."

Every player may feel the same way, but Jordan's ability to convert the sensation into scoring huge goals is why big things are expected from him for a long time to come.

★★★★★★★★★★★★★★★★★★★★★★★★★★★★★★★★★★

JORDAN EBERLE'S FAVORITE [...] GROWING UP

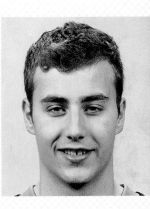

PLAYERS: PAVEL BURE AND JOE SAKIC
MUSICIANS: NICKELBACK, KENNY CHESNEY AND THEORY OF A DEAD MAN
MOVIE: *THE HANGOVER*
VIDEO GAME: EA SPORTS NHL SERIES
SPORT OTHER THAN HOCKEY: GOLF
SUBJECT: PHYS-ED AND MATH

★★★★★★★★★★★★★★★★★★★★★★★★★★★★★★★★★★

149

ERIK JOHNSON

COLORADO AVALANCHE

POSITION: DEFENSE
DRAFTED: 1ST OVERALL IN 2006
BORN: MARCH 21, 1988 – BLOOMINGTON, MINN.
LAST DEVELOPMENTAL TEAM: MINNESOTA GOLDEN GOPHERS (WCHA)

The folklore around grassroots hockey often involves kids and their parents getting up at 6 a.m. on the weekend, driving down to the local rink and piling out onto the ice to play the game they love. But for Colorado defenseman Erik Johnson, the story would have been so much better if he only could have slept in a few hours later.

"I can remember taking him to the rink when he was six years old, kicking and screaming," said Bruce Johnson, Erik's dad. "He loved it. He just didn't like getting up early."

Once the Bloomington, Minn., native got on the ice, though, it was a different story.

"My goal was to skate around the faceoff circle without falling," Erik said.

Growing up in the State of Hockey, it was impossible to avoid a love for the game and Erik was no exception. According to his dad, Erik practically lived in the garage, shooting pucks and wheeling around on his rollerblades. When he needed a live target to shoot on, the unfortunate job fell to his younger sister, Christina.

"She had to be the goalie more often than not," Bruce said. "A lot of times she came in crying."

> **"I can remember taking Erik to the rink when he was six years old, kicking and screaming. He loved it. He just didn't like getting up early."**
>
> **– Bruce Johnson**

150

When it came to playing competitively, Erik wanted to take things slow and his parents were more than happy to oblige him.

"There was a higher level he could have played, but he didn't feel ready for it," Bruce said. "We weren't putting him on a pedestal at a young age."

But the company Erik would keep turned out to be a pretty good indicator of where he was headed in life. In Minnesota, there was youth hockey in the winter and then AAA hockey in the summer. Essentially, the best players from the winter would come together on one team when the weather got nicer. From the time Erik was 10 until he was 15, his summer mates comprised a Bloomington-Jefferson team that was veritable murderer's row of future stars.

Avalanche teammate Peter Mueller, Carolina's Jamie McBain and New York Islanders power forward Kyle Okposo were all on that summer squad, as was Nashville pick Ryan Flynn and Colorado prospect Mike Carman.

"That is pretty amazing if you think about it," Erik said.

Members of that squad would also eventually make their mark locally. Every player mentioned went on to play at the University of Minnesota, with the exception of McBain, who attended the rival University of Wisconsin and Peter Mueller, who played in the Western League for the Everett Silvertips. The Golden Gophers have always been a Minnesota institution, but even more so when Erik was young. The North Stars left town in 1993 and the Wild didn't hit the ice until 2000.

"Growing up, I didn't have an NHL team to follow," he said. "So I was a big Gophers fan."

Luckily for Erik, the Gophers were also big fans of him. According to Bruce, Erik was already 6-foot-2 and 185 pounds by the time he was 14. That's when the University of Minnesota came calling.

"That was the most shocking of anything," Bruce said.

Traditionally in Minnesota, kids play high school hockey right up until university, where the Gophers dominate, but also get competition from Minnesota-Duluth, Minnesota State-Mankato and St. Cloud State (not to mention Wisconsin). But Erik had a different choice in mind as he prepped for his time with the Gophers: Team USA's national

151

DESPITE BEING A NO. 1
OVERALL DRAFT PICK,
ERIK JOHNSON WAS
TRADED BY ST. LOUIS
TO COLORADO. HE NOW
USES THAT AS
MOTIVATION TO PLAY
EVEN BETTER.

team development program in Ann Arbor, Mich., which had approached him and his parents when he played in a Selects-15 tournament.

"When I look back on it, it was a pretty big moment," Erik said. "There were no ifs, ands or buts. I was going to go, no matter what my parents said. I needed that structure and it gave me a path to the NHL."

Looking into the program, Erik's parents were satisfied their son would get the guidance he needed off the ice, trusting a program that was far from home.

"Frankly, we were more worried about the kid side than the hockey side," Bruce said. "Erik made it very clear that this is what he wanted to do. We came away extremely pleased with USA Hockey."

Erik's time in Ann Arbor was very productive. He spent two seasons with the program, winning gold at the under-18s in his first campaign and another in his second season. In the second tournament he placed second in defenseman scoring with 10 points in six games, one behind his buddy McBain. Erik also made the jump to the world juniors that year, experiencing the big-stage hype of a major tournament held in Canada. It was in Vancouver that Erik learned something else: He was the favorite to go first overall in the 2006 NHL draft.

"I didn't even really know it was my draft year," he said. "I had never watched TSN before and then I turned it on in Vancouver and they were talking about me."

It all started to snowball after that. Erik's ultimate goal had been to play for the Gophers, but now he was being considered the best in his age group in the world. Sure enough, when the day came, the St. Louis Blues tabbed Erik with the top pick.

"Even to this day it's hard to describe," Bruce said. "It came out of nowhere. I'm sure Troy Crosby was thinking about Sidney going first years in advance, but we had no clue."

Unlike most first overall picks, Erik wasn't rushed by the Blues. In fact, he became the first player since Ottawa's Chris Phillips in

> "I didn't even really know it was my draft year. I had never watched TSN before and then I turned it on and they were talking about me."
>
> **— Erik Johnson**

153

1996 not to go straight to the NHL. It was a move that was fine by Erik, to be sure.

"That was the only thing I wanted to do as a kid," he said of his freshman campaign at Minnesota. "To put on that uniform and skate around Mariucci Arena for a year was amazing."

The next season, the NHL came calling. A foot injury shortened his rookie run, but Erik still finished with five goals and 33 points in 69 games. It was a great start for a young defenseman on a rebuilding team. But a cruel twist would derail Erik's progress.

As the 2008-09 season was just about to get underway, Erik was involved in an accident with a golf cart at a team function. He sustained a knee injury serious enough to require surgery and missed the entire season. Even though St. Louis had been a long shot in the West, the Blues managed to sneak into the post-season before being swept by the Canucks. It was a tough time for Erik, but he wasn't alone.

"I view my job as a parent to be a stabilizing influence, to keep him level," Bruce said. "Certainly the knee injury was difficult, but I've always tried to keep his head on square."

Erik returned the next season in fine form, suiting up for all but three games while doubling his rookie goal output and increasing his point total to 39. On top of that, he was honored with a spot on Team USA's Olympic squad, which famously fought Canada for gold, only to come out on the losing end in overtime.

But the surprises didn't end there for Erik. Two-thirds of the way through the 2010-11 season he was part of a blockbuster trade between St. Louis and Colorado. Erik, veteran Jay McClement and a first round pick (which turned out to be another big defenseman, Duncan Siemens) headed to the Avalanche in exchange for power forward Chris Stewart, blueliner Kevin Shattenkirk and a second round selection (right winger Ty Rattie).

Needless to say, it was an unexpected move.

"St. Louis, I pretty much spent four full years there," Erik said. "You come to like a city and it's tough to leave."

While the emerging Blues had run into injury problems that season and underwhelmed, the Avs were in full-on rebuild mode, so expectations were lower. Erik came into a situation where defense was going to be a soft spot, since veteran Adam Foote had retired and the team would see power play stalwart John-Michael Liles exit via free agency in the summer. Plus, of course, Shattenkirk had gone the other way to St. Louis.

Fortunately, the pressure is something Erik enjoys.

"Coming to a young team, hopefully I can be a stabilizing force on the blueline," he said. "The biggest thing is Colorado wanted me."

No surprise there. Erik is, after all, a 6-foot-4, 236-pound force with room to grow as a player. Defensemen tend to take a little longer to develop and with the knee surgery erasing an entire campaign, it's fair to say Erik's best is yet to come.

And if everything goes as the Avs and Johnson hope, it'll be the management team in St. Louis who will end up kicking and screaming over their decision to deal him away.

★★★★★★★★★★★★★★★★★★★★★★★★★★★★★★★★★

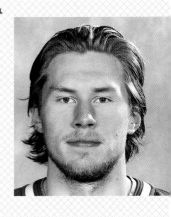

ERIK JOHNSON'S FAVORITE [...] GROWING UP

JERSEYS: VANCOUVER CANUCKS AND FLORIDA PANTHERS (PAVEL BURE)
MEMORABILIA: PERSONALIZED BOBBY ORR PHOTO AND STICK SIGNED BY U.S. OLYMPIC TEAM
CARTOON: RUGRATS
ALBUM: GREATEST HITS BY TOBY KEITH
VIDEO GAME: NHL '94 FOR SEGA GENESIS
SCHOOL SUBJECT: HISTORY
JUNK FOOD: BROWNIES

★★★★★★★★★★★★★★★★★★★★★★★★★★★★★★★★★

P.K. SUBBAN

MONTREAL CANADIENS

POSITION: DEFENSE
DRAFTED: 43RD OVERALL IN 2007
BORN: MAY 13, 1989 – TORONTO, ONT.
LAST DEVELOPMENTAL TEAM: BELLEVILLE BULLS (OHL)

A lot of things come naturally to P.K. Subban.

For starters, the guy is definitely a talker. And though that's been known to ruffle a few feathers, his bold personality is also very engaging and devoid of fabrication.

But it may come as a surprise to some who've seen him whip down the ice with a strong skating stride or fire a first-rate slapshot to the back of the net that P.K.'s emergence as one of the most dynamic young defensemen in the game is owed far more to sweat than skill.

The work ethic is easily traced to his father, Karl Subban.

"Maybe it's my teaching background," said Karl, the principal of Brookview Middle School in Toronto. "If you want to be good at something you start young and practise frequently and good things will happen."

Karl (P.K. is Pernell Karl) immigrated to frigid Sudbury, Ont., from sunny Jamaica with his family at the age of 11. Growing up in a francophone neighborhood, Karl quickly absorbed the love of hockey emanating from other kids on his street. His affection for the sport only grew when he began attending Ontario League Sudbury Wolves games and watching the Montreal Canadiens on TV.

When it came time to start his teaching career, Karl moved to Toronto, where he and wife Maria have raised five children. The girls, Nastassia and Natasha, came first, then P.K. started a trend of hockey-playing boys, with Malcolm and Jordan to follow.

By the time he was two-and-a-half, P.K. was on skates.

"He was still in Pampers when he started," Karl said.

P.K.'s trips with his dad to a downtown Toronto outdoor ice pad as a very young boy have already started to become part of Canadian hockey lore.

Karl, setting the tone of hard work, was basically pulling two teaching shifts daily, the first as an administrator, then as VP of a continuing education program in the evening. Most people would be dreaming of a pillow instead of an ice pad after logging those hours, but Karl would walk through the door to find P.K. asleep in his snow pants.

"He was still in Pampers when he started skating."

– Karl Subban

"He'd come home and wake me up and take me down to Nathan Phillips Square," P.K. said. "I'd be skating until one or two o'clock in the morning."

Because he was young enough that he only attended school in the afternoon, P.K. was free to rest up in the morning. Karl has joked in the past that their seemingly excessive regimen wasn't child abuse, it was just something they both loved to do. And for all the talk of dedication and work, Karl always found ways to reward his son.

"After every skate he'd take me for a treat, a pizza slice or something like that," P.K. said.

Karl began making a rink in the backyard of the family home and soon, with Malcolm and Jordan following their big brother's strides, it was a hive of activity.

"We'd be out there for hours and I never once complained, I loved to do it," P.K. said. "I have tons of memories of those skates."

P.K.'s rise through the minor hockey ranks eventually led him to the Ontario League's Belleville Bulls, though he was a sixth round pick in his draft year of 2005. By his own admission, P.K. had a lot of learning and growing to do at that stage of his career, both on and off the ice. Luckily, Bulls coach George Burnett was the perfect tutor.

"Not only did he groom me as a player, he groomed me as a person," P.K. said. "I left Belleville a lot more mature, a lot more ready. I was just a better person all around."

Both Malcolm and Jordan also know first-hand what P.K. is talking about. Malcolm is a Bulls goalie eligible for the 2012 NHL draft and Jordan, a defenseman, was selected fifth overall by the Belleville squad in the summer of 2011 and is set to carve out his major junior career.

"There's no other place I'd rather have them because I know what George did for me," P.K. said.

After his second year in Belleville, P.K. was drafted in the second round, 43rd overall, by the Canadiens, meaning he was on his way to playing for the team both he and his dad grew up rooting for. It also meant that, while he still wasn't a high selection, P.K.'s stock had climbed from being a late-round OHL pick to a second-rounder in the NHL.

"It's not the round you go in, it's the round you come out," Karl said with a chuckle. "Someone said that to me and I haven't forgotten that."

It was during his junior career that P.K. gained Canada-wide notoriety after he won back-to-back gold medals at the 2008 and '09 World Junior Championships. At his first tournament, P.K. went pointless in seven games. But during his second event, held in the Canadian capital of Ottawa, he was a star, sniping nine points in six games to lead Canada to a fifth-straight gold medal.

His flare-infused style and take-charge attitude on an international stage may have helped obscure the fact P.K. has had to hustle every step of the way. No doubt every player who makes the NHL, regardless of how talented he is, must put in the work, but P.K. believes that element of his ascent is sometimes glossed over.

"What a lot of people don't talk about is the fact I went to Hamilton (of the American League) and I rode the bus for a year and I paid my dues," he said. "I wasn't a top-five pick who cruised into the NHL."

It was during his rookie pro season of 2009-10 with the Hamilton Bulldogs that P.K. made his NHL debut, a two-game cameo with the Habs. Then, in the spring of 2010, P.K. joined the Canadiens during their run to the Eastern Conference final, playing a prominent role on the blueline for 14 playoff games after the team lost No. 1 defenseman Andrei Markov to injury.

P.K. SUBBAN'S MOUTH
HAS GOT HIM IN HOT
WATER A COUPLE OF
TIMES IN HIS YOUNG
CAREER. BUT HIS
SIZZLING PLAY IS ALL
FANS IN MONTREAL
CARE ABOUT.

Expectations were high for P.K. the following fall in his rookie season, but when his risk-reward radar became skewed, coach Jacques Martin decided to make him a healthy scratch for a few games. However, in the second half of the year, with Montreal's blueline again decimated by injuries, P.K. found his form and became a leading member of the 'D' corps.

Along the way, his brazen approach and theatrical celebrations prompted some members of the hockey community to suggest a rookie shouldn't carry himself in that manner.

"I think the people who know me know I'm humble," he said. "I'm confident and I'll never back down from anybody and I'm going to speak my mind because that's what I've been taught. But I respect the game, I respect my teammates, I respect my opponents. When it comes to playing the game, I'm just very competitive."

> ### "I'm going to speak my mind because that's what I've been taught. But I respect the game, I respect my teammates, I respect my opponents."
>
> ## — P.K. Subban

P.K. concluded his freshman season with 38 points in 77 games, good for third amongst first-year defensemen. His strong overall play down the stretch also earned him a selection to the NHL's all-rookie team.

Along with young goalie Carey Price, P.K. is seen as a cornerstone of the Montreal franchise, a player who will be counted on to contribute points, hits and "holy cow!" moments for years to come. P.K. is well aware how intense the glare in Montreal can be, but true to his confident nature he's ready to face things head-on.

"I'd be crazy not to relish that," he said of the pressure. "This is the most storied franchise in hockey history."

Of course, the reward for a job well done with the red, white and blue would go well beyond the slice of pizza P.K. used to get from his dad after their late-night skates.

And if one thing can be gleaned from P.K.'s career to this point, he's definitely willing to use some elbow grease in pursuit of his goals.

"I remember when he was running the hills, I used to say, 'P.K., there's a kid in Sweden, there's a kid in Russia who's probably sleeping now and you're working hard'," Karl said. "That was like a motivating thing.

"You've got to work for what you want in life and he's certainly learned his lessons well." – *Ryan Dixon*

★★★★★★★★★★★★★★★★★★★★★★★★★★★★★★★★★★

P.K. SUBBAN'S FAVORITE [...] GROWING UP

PLAYER: BOBBY ORR
JERSEY: MONTREAL CANADIENS
CARTOON: POWER RANGERS
MOVIE: GLADIATOR
VIDEO GAME: SUPER MARIO BROS.
SPORTS OTHER THAN HOCKEY: SOCCER AND BASKETBALL
SCHOOL SUBJECT: ART

★★★★★★★★★★★★★★★★★★★★★★★★★★★★★★★★★★

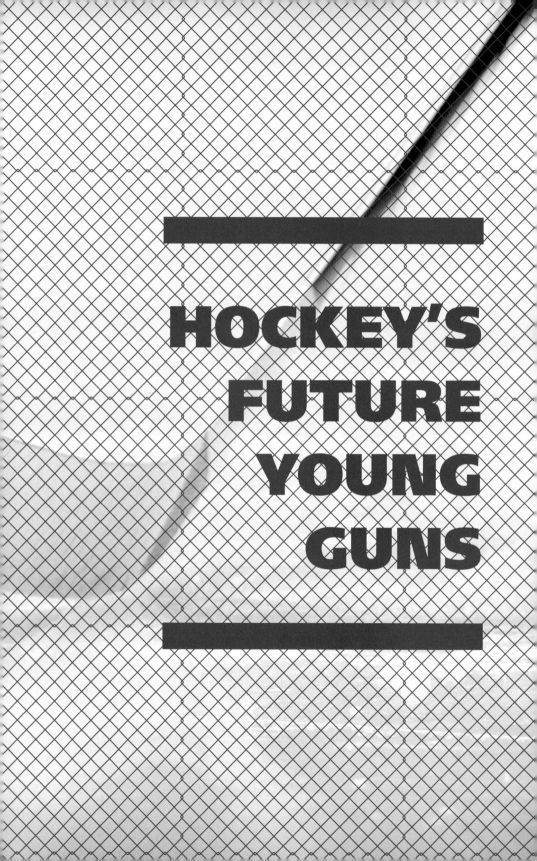

HOCKEY'S FUTURE YOUNG GUNS

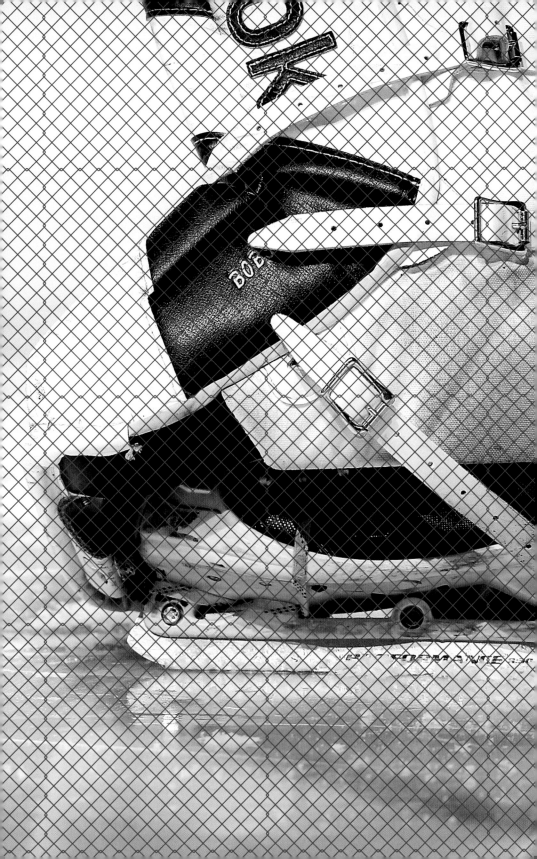

RYAN NUGENT-HOPKINS

POSITION: CENTER
DRAFTED: 1ST OVERALL IN 2011
BORN: APRIL 12, 1993 – BURNABY, B.C.
LAST DEVELOPMENTAL TEAM: RED DEER REBELS (WHL)

Ryan Nugent-Hopkins will soon join an Edmonton Oilers squad with a bevy of young talent. And if history is an indicator he may very well end up the best of the lot.

Nugent-Hopkins played minor hockey for the Burnaby Winter Club and led his bantam team to a Western Canadian title. Things kept going uphill from there, as Nugent-Hopkins was selected first overall in the Western League bantam draft by the Red Deer Rebels in 2008.

The next season, he was a force playing AAA midget in Vancouver. His 87 points in 36 games earned him B.C.'s minor player of the year award. When his midget team was bounced from the playoffs, the six-foot, 171-pound center was called up to the Rebels lineup as an underager and made an immediate impact. In only five games, he tallied two goals and six points.

In his rookie campaign with the Rebels in 2009-10, 'The Nuge' notched 24 goals and 65 points in 67 games. At the end of the season he was named WHL rookie of the year and also a finalist for CHL rookie of the year honors, claimed by Peterborough Pete and 2011 Ottawa Senators draft pick Matt Puempel.

Nugent-Hopkins' sophomore year with the Rebels was explosive. He had 106 points in 67 games, prompting the Oilers to take him first overall. His vision and hockey sense are so outstanding some observers have drawn comparisons to Pavel Datsyuk or even 'The Great One,' Wayne Gretzky.

The Burnaby, B.C., native has displayed his wizardry on the international scene, too. He played for Team Pacific at the 2010 Under-17 World Hockey Challenge and led Canada to gold at the 2010 Ivan Hlinka Memorial Tournament in Slovakia, where he scored the winning goal in the gold medal game.

With Taylor Hall, Jordan Eberle and Magnus Paajarvi already on the scene, the Oilers future looks bright. Throw Nugent-Hopkins in the mix and it's easy to understand why Edmonton fans are giddy over what's around the corner.
– *Connie Jensen*

RYAN NUGENT-HOPKINS WILL HAVE TO GET STRONGER BEFORE HE'S READY TO DOMINATE THE NHL…AND HELP CARRY THE EXPECTATIONS OF A CITY USED TO SEEING THEIR TEAM HOIST CUPS.

TYLER SEGUIN

BOSTON BRUINS

POSITION: CENTER
DRAFTED: 2ND OVERALL IN 2010
BORN: JANUARY 31, 1992 – BRAMPTON, ONT.
LAST DEVELOPMENTAL TEAM: PLYMOUTH WHALERS (OHL)

It wasn't long ago Tyler Seguin was looking forward to being one of the top picks in the NHL draft. Now, he's a Stanley Cup champion.

Seguin was a star from the time he started playing hockey in Whitby, Ont., when he was five years old. Throughout his minor hockey career he was teammates with players who have already made their mark in the NHL. In his Ontario League draft year, while playing with the Toronto Young Nationals, he was linemates with Carolina Hurricanes center and 2011 Calder Trophy winner Jeff Skinner. Also on that squad was Jamie Oleksiak, who was drafted in the first round by the Dallas Stars in 2011.

Seguin was drafted ninth overall by the Plymouth Whalers in 2008 and was a star during his OHL career, scoring 173 points in 124 games. He topped it off by winning the Red Tilson Trophy as the most outstanding player during his final junior campaign.

The Boston Bruins selected the Brampton, Ont., native with the second overall pick in the 2010 draft. In his freshman season, Seguin finished with a respectable 22 points in 74 games, putting him 22nd in rookie scoring.

During the playoffs, Seguin was scratched for the first two rounds. He was finally given an opportunity to step into the lineup during the Eastern Conference final and it was an opportunity he would not waste. He dominated play right off the hop, scoring six points in his first two games and ultimately helping Boston to the title. Fans finally got a taste of the unlimited potential he has.

The Cup is already his. Tyler Seguin now has the rest of his career to etch his own name into history. *– Adam Scully*

AFTER A HO-HUM REGULAR SEASON, TYLER SEGUIN BROKE OUT DURING THE BRUINS STANLEY CUP RUN IN 2011. NOW HE'LL BE EXPECTED TO EARN STRAIGHT A'S FOR THE B'S ON A REGULAR BASIS.

TYLER ENNIS

BUFFALO SABRES

POSITION: LEFT WING
DRAFTED: 26TH OVERALL IN 2008
BORN: OCTOBER 6, 1989 – EDMONTON, ALTA.
LAST DEVELOPMENTAL TEAM: MEDICINE HAT TIGERS (WHL)

Ten years ago, the diminutive Tyler Ennis may not have even been given a shot at the NHL. Now, he's not even the smallest player on his team.

That honor goes to 5-foot-5 Nathan Gerbe, but at 5-foot-9, Ennis is no colossus himself. What he is, though, is an integral part of the Buffalo Sabres' present and future.

As a member of the Western League's Medicine Hat Tigers, Ennis carved up the competition, posting back-to-back 43-goal campaigns and earning first-team WHL East all-star nods both times. In 2009, he also helped Canada win gold on home soil in Ottawa at the World Junior Championship, with seven points in six games.

But it was his introduction to the NHL that really set the stage.

In his first game as a Sabre, Ennis scored against Philadelphia. That was as an emergency injury call-up, but the Sabres brought Ennis back from American League Portland for the stretch drive. In the final nine games of the season he registered eight points, helping Buffalo to the 2010 Northeast Division title.

A first round matchup against Boston ended in defeat, but Ennis was the Sabres' best player, whirling around giant defenseman Zdeno Chara and not backing down when the behemoth Norris Trophy winner snarled. He also tied for the Sabres lead in scoring with four points in six contests.

In Ennis' first full NHL campaign, he hit the 20-goal mark and suited up in all 82 games for Buffalo.

Big heart in a little frame – seems to have worked out just fine for the kid. – *Ryan Kennedy*

TYLER ENNIS, ALONG WITH FELLOW SHORTY NATHAN GERBE, HAS ADDED A NEW ELEMENT OF SPEED AND SKILL TO THE BUFFALO SABRES.

JACOB MARKSTROM

FLORIDA PANTHERS

POSITION: GOALIE

DRAFTED: 31ST OVERALL IN 2008

BORN: JANUARY 31, 1990 – GAVLE, SWEDEN

LAST DEVELOPMENTAL TEAM: BRYNAS IF GAVLE (SWEDEN)

Becoming an NHL starting netminder is hard enough, but for Jacob Markstrom, he carries the added pressure of being dubbed the top goaltending prospect in the world and future savior of the Florida Panthers.

That'd be too daunting for most, but that pressure has been part of everyday life since Markstrom was just 18 years old and he's handled it well at every step.

Markstrom's coming-out party came during the 2009 World Junior Championship in Ottawa. By posting a 1.61 goals-against average and a .943 save percentage, he led Sweden to a silver medal and was given the tournament's top goaltender award for his efforts.

Markstrom's transition to the pro game was seamless. In his first full season in the Swedish Elite League with Brynas, Markstrom frustrated shooters en route to recording a 2.38 goals-against average and a .917 save percentage. He only improved from there in 2009-10 when he posted a 2.01 GAA and .927 SP, earning him the SEL goalie of the year award.

The youngster crossed the Atlantic during the fall of 2010 to join Florida's then-American League affiliate, the Rochester Americans. While he struggled in adapting to North American hockey early in the year, he regained his dominant form after 20 games before a knee injury ended his season.

Even though he has just begun of his NHL career, Markstrom is at the forefront of a new wave of Swedish goaltending talent coming over here. If his trophy case is any indication of his future, look for Markstrom to pocket a Vezina or two before his career is over. – *Chris Lund*

THE PANTHERS ARE A TEAM WHO'VE BEEN KNOWN FOR SOLID GOALTENDING (UNFORTUNATELY, LITTLE ELSE) AND JACOB MARKSTROM IS SURE TO CONTINUE THAT TREND ONCE HE TAKES OVER AS NO. 1.

ADAM LARSSON

NEW JERSEY DEVILS

POSITION: DEFENSE

DRAFTED: 4TH OVERALL IN 2011

BORN: NOVEMBER 12, 1992 – SKELLEFTEA, SWEDEN

LAST DEVELOPMENTAL TEAM: SKELLEFTEA HC (SWEDEN)

Adam Larsson prides himself on being a cool customer on the ice, a blueliner who doesn't get rattled and plays as if the game has slowed down in front of him. But there was a crack in that cool just after he was selected at the 2011 draft by New Jersey.

When asked what it would be like to play in front of iconic goaltender Martin Brodeur, the 6-foot-3, 197-pound Swede let a grin crack across his face and began to half-giggle at his own good fortune. Though he had slipped to fourth in the draft, he was going to a team with three Stanley Cups in the past 15 seasons and a lineup dotted with stars.

But on a squad historically known for defense, New Jersey was bereft of blueline talent when Larsson arrived, so his future opportunities were gold.

The big kid from Skelleftea cut his teeth in the Swedish Elite League, playing two seasons against competition that was sometimes a decade or more older than him. In that time, he established himself as a two-way threat and helped his squad to the league final in 2011.

Larsson's coming-out party for North Americans occurred at the 2011 World Junior Championship in Buffalo with dominating performances in losing causes against Russia and the United States in the medal round.

While Brodeur's career is in its twilight, Larsson's time in New Jersey is just beginning. – *Ryan Kennedy*

A GREAT DEAL OF EXPERIENCE IN SWEDEN'S TOP LEAGUE AND THE WORLD JUNIORS MADE ADAM LARSSON A COOL CUSTOMER HEADING INTO THE NHL.

GABRIEL LANDESKOG

COLORADO AVALANCHE

POSITION: LEFT WING
DRAFTED: 2ND OVERALL IN 2011
BORN: NOVEMBER 23, 1992 – STOCKHOLM, SWEDEN
LAST DEVELOPMENTAL TEAM: KITCHENER RANGERS (OHL)

When a European player first comes to North America, there is usually a steep learning curve, both on and off the ice. For Gabriel Landeskog, the transition has been seamless.

The Stockholm, Sweden native has been learning the English language since he was in Grade 3 and he plays a North American-style game that translates well to the NHL. During his first season with the Ontario League's Kitchener Rangers, Landeskog had 46 points in 61 games. He exploded during the playoffs, however, scoring 23 points in 20 contests.

His play didn't go unnoticed.

Early on in his second season he was given the ultimate compliment. At the tender age of 17, Landeskog was named captain of the Rangers, becoming the first European to wear the 'C' in their storied history.

The youngster has drawn a lot of comparison to L.A. Kings center (and fellow former Kitchener captain) Mike Richards.

Many scouts dubbed Landeskog the most NHL-ready player in the 2011 draft class. Colorado snagged him with the second overall pick.

Landeskog has already joined other members of the Avalanche who made the jump straight from junior to the NHL. After the 2009 draft, 18-year-olds Matt Duchene and Ryan O'Reilly made the rare leap.

Expect Landeskog's next seamless transition to be into NHL stardom. – *Adam Scully*

GABRIEL LANDESKOG'S LEADERSHIP QUALITIES MADE HIM THE FIRST EUROPEAN CAPTAIN THE KITCHENER RANGERS EVER HAD. COLORADO TOOK HIM SECOND OVERALL IN 2011.

ERIK GUDBRANSON

FLORIDA PANTHERS

POSITION: DEFENSE
DRAFTED: 3RD OVERALL IN 2010
BORN: JANUARY 7, 1992 – ORLEANS, ONTARIO
LAST DEVELOPMENTAL TEAM: KINGSTON FRONTENACS (OHL)

Being in the top-five is something Erik Gudbranson is used to.

In 2008, after playing minor hockey for the Gloucester Rangers and the Ottawa Junior 67's, Gudbranson was drafted fourth overall by the Kingston Frontenacs and headed just down the road from where he grew up to start his major junior career.

The 6-foot-4, 195-pounder has a resume that's nearly as imposing as his frame. He captained Team Ontario's gold medal-winning under-17 squad in 2009 and earned spots on Canada's under-18 team in 2009 and 2010, as well as the world juniors squad that took home silver in 2011.

The strong blueliner's NHL dreams came true when he went third overall in 2010 to the Florida Panthers. With so many critical components to his game already in place, many believed Gudbranson was ready to make the jump to the NHL right after the draft. However, he couldn't come to terms on a contract with the Panthers and returned to Kingston.

The additional junior season seemed to be both a blessing and a curse for the big man. On one hand, he hit new levels of productivity with 12 goals and 34 points in just 44 games. On the other, Gudbranson picked up three separate suspensions totalling 14 games (two for rambunctious play and the other for an internal issue with his team).

Florida GM Dale Tallon inked his first draft pick with the organization to a contract in July of 2011. From being drafted fourth overall in the OHL to No. 3 in the big show, Gudbranson is now set to embark on a career path where he's expected to develop into the No. 1 defenseman and anchor the Florida blueline for years to come.

– *Connie Jensen*

FLORIDA FANS ARE JUST LEARNING NOW THE SWEET AND SOUR SIDES OF ERIK GUDBRANSON AFTER A CONTRACT DISPUTE PUT HIM BACK IN JUNIOR FOR 2010-11.

ALEXANDER BURMISTROV

POSITION: CENTER
DRAFTED: 8TH OVERALL IN 2010
BORN: OCTOBER 21, 1991 – KAZAN, RUSSIA
LAST DEVELOPMENTAL TEAM: BARRIE COLTS (OHL)

When Alexander Burmistrov landed in North America, he was so skinny it looked like a stiff wind could blow him over. Not much has changed since then, except the fact the brainy young Russian was good enough to jump straight from the draft to the NHL and not look out of place in the process.

Burmistrov's North American career started in 2009-10 with the Ontario League's Barrie Colts. The team was a powerhouse that season, going all the way to the OHL final before losing to Windsor. Burmistrov helped out along the way by killing penalties, quarterbacking the power play's second unit and putting up numbers at a point-per-game pace.

Despite his slender six-foot, 170-pound frame, he was tough to knock off the puck and valued as one of the smartest players in the draft by a panel of scouts.

The consensus among pundits was Burmistrov, who went eighth overall in the 2010 draft, needed more development before making the jump to the NHL. But there he was on opening night in Atlanta, winning 60 percent of his draws against the powerhouse Capitals, then scoring his first pro goal in his 10th game, against the Sabres. The Russian pivot ended up with six goals and 20 points in 74 games for a fine rookie season on a Thrashers squad that missed the playoffs.

Based on his skill set and his quick progression, it's fair to say the fans in Winnipeg will be happy to see this Jet on their runway for years to come. – *Ryan Kennedy*

ALEXANDER BURMISTROV RAISED SOME EYEBROWS WHEN HE MADE THE THRASHERS RIGHT AFTER BEING SELECTED EIGHTH OVERALL IN THE 2010 DRAFT. NOW THE SLICK RUSSIAN TAKES HIS GAME UP NORTH TO SEE IF HE CAN TAKE OFF WITH THE JETS.

KEVIN SHATTENKIRK

ST. LOUIS BLUES

POSITION: DEFENSE
DRAFTED: 14TH OVERALL IN 2007
BORN: JANUARY 29, 1989 – GREENWICH, CONN.
LAST DEVELOPMENTAL TEAM: BOSTON UNIVERSITY (NCAA)

If a team is willing to trade its franchise defenseman for you just shy of 50 games into your career, you must be pretty good. That's exactly what happened to Kevin Shattenkirk during his rookie season in 2010-11, when he and Colorado teammate Chris Stewart went to St. Louis in exchange for Erik Johnson, the first overall pick from 2006. Now with the Blues, Shattenkirk is a cornerstone of one of the NHL's most exciting young defense corps.

With plenty of skill at his disposal, Shattenkirk has been ahead of his class since his teenage years. At the 2007 World Under-18 Championship, he captained Team USA to a silver medal and was named the tournament's best defenseman. The following summer the Avs made Shattenkirk their first draft choice, 14th overall.

Since then Shattenkirk has played in the World Junior Championship, set up the tournament-winning goal at the 2009 NCAA Frozen Four, became Boston University's first junior captain since 1962 and made his national team debut at the 2011 World Championship. Not too shabby when you consider he did it all before his 23rd birthday.

During his successful rookie campaign, Shattenkirk tallied 43 points in just 72 games to lead all first-year defensemen in scoring. His performance earned him a spot as one of the 12 rookies selected to the NHL All-Star Game weekend.

Even though he is still refining his game, Shattenkirk has been compared favorably to three-time Stanley Cup champion Brian Rafalski, who recently retired after a very distinguished and successful career as one of the better American defensemen to play the game.

Look for Shattenkirk, a solid puck-mover who packs a strong shot, and Alex Pietrangelo, a fellow St. Louis top-pair blueliner, to have opposing goalies singing the Blues for many years to come. – *Chris Lund*

BEING PART OF DEAL THAT SAW A NO. 1 PICK GO THE OTHER WAY CAN BE A LOT OF PRESSURE, BUT IF KEVIN SHATTENKIRK CONTINUES HIS ASCENT IN ST. LOUIS ALL BLUES' FANS WILL BE PLEASED.

NINO NIEDERREITER

POSITION: RIGHT WING
DRAFTED: 5TH OVERALL IN 2010
BORN: SEPTEMBER 8, 1992 – CHUR, SWITZERLAND
LAST DEVELOPMENTAL TEAM: PORTLAND WINTER HAWKS (WHL)

A funny thing happened at the 2010 World Junior Championship in Saskatoon, Sask.

While the Canadians once again played for a gold medal and were joined in the final four by Team USA and Sweden, the last entry in the quartet was not Russia or Finland or even the Czechs or Slovaks – it was Switzerland. And the Swiss earned it, largely on the backs of goaltender Benjamin Conz and right winger Nino Niederreiter.

'El Nino' dazzled in the medal round, willing his team to a huge victory over the Russians in the quarterfinal by tallying both the game-tying goal in the last minute of play, then the overtime winner as the Swiss recorded a fantastic 3-2 triumph over one of hockey's great powers.

With a combination of physical might, nifty skill and a flare of drama, Niederreiter became an instant hero. All told, the right winger rang up six goals and 10 points in seven games to lead the Swiss squad.

Niederreiter was already a great contributor for the Western League's Portland Winterhawks, so it was no surprise to folks in the PDX. At the 2010 draft later that summer, he was selected fifth overall by the Islanders, one pick after linemate Ryan Johansen, who went to Columbus.

In 2011, Niederreiter not only helped the Winterhawks to the WHL final, but also acted as a mentor to countryman Sven Bartschi, who parlayed his excellent work into a first round selection by Calgary.

Niederreiter is part of a great crop of young forwards being harvested on Long Island, so the headlines won't stop coming anytime soon. – *Ryan Kennedy*